Praise for
Transforming the Healthcare Experience through the Arts

"Arts projects and programs are not architectural add-ons or fringe niceties. They are an essential part of core design and dramatically affect patient care outcomes. This book makes a major contribution to the developing literature on evidence based environmental design. In addition, it is fun to read and is beautifully illustrated. Hats off to Blair Sadler and Annette Ridenour! They have given us a work that is destined to become a classic in the literature of healthcare."

– from the Foreword by **Leland R. Kaiser**, Ph.D., Health Futurist

"This deeply important and inspiring book will broaden your horizons and lift your spirits. During the endless debates about 'reform,' it reminds us what we really want from our healthcare system to make it truly patient-centered."

– **Donald M. Berwick**, President and CEO, Institute for Healthcare Improvement

"A compelling journey into the healing power of art. A beautiful book physically and in the inspiring story it tells."

– **Leonard L. Berry**, Ph.D., co-author of *Management Lessons from Mayo Clinic* and Distinguished Professor of Marketing, Mays Business School, Texas A&M University

"Why should you read *Transforming the Healthcare Experience through the Arts*? For the possibility of saving billions of dollars by not having to sedate children facing MRIs or CAT scans? For the experience of meeting artists such as photographer Jeff Dykehouse, whose portraits of dying children and their families are precious gifts beyond price? Or for its profound insights into what gives our lives their shape and meaning? Whatever your reasons, if you care about health, hospitals, caregivers, and patients, read this book."

– **Thomas H. Murray**, Ph.D., President and CEO, The Hastings Center

"In this elegant and inspirational, book, Blair Sadler and Annette Ridenour have shown that it is not only desirable but absolutely essential to bring the Arts and the Sciences together if we are to meet the challenge of designing and developing better healthcare systems. Like all good designers, healthcare improvement leaders and facilitators need to think 'both-and' as scientists and artists. This book will show them what they need to do and how to do it. Above all, it will inspire them to want to go out and do it. Hopefully, the book will also tempt more of our talented artists and designers to want to come and work in partnership with healthcare providers and users to transform the healthcare experience."

– **Paul Bate**, Emeritus Professor of Healthcare Management, The Medical School, University College London

"Never has there been a more stunning, inspiring and artistic contribution to the arts in modern healthcare. This book sets a new standard with the use of sound, sight, and environment through its clinical foundation and visionary beauty. Annette Ridenour and Blair Sadler lead the field in bringing a world of harmony to healthcare."

– **Don Campbell**, author of *The Harmony of Health; Music: Physician for Times to Come;* and *The Mozart Effect*®

"The Sadler Awards generously recognize excellence in the arts associated with healthcare. Now Blair Sadler and Annette Ridenour have documented the case for the importance of the full and rich range of the arts in healthcare settings, and they have compiled a fabulous and extensive first-of-its-kind collection of art resources for enlightened healthcare organizations and their design teams. Anyone with a role in health facility décor and design should have this helpful book at their side."

– **D. Kirk Hamilton**, Co-Editor, Health Environments Research and Design Journal

"This well organized, well written, and beautifully illustrated book merits serious consideration for selection as assigned reading in schools of architecture, design, medicine, nursing, and healthcare administration. Congratulations to Blair Sadler and Annette Ridenour for providing this valuable contribution that can help improve the healthcare experiences of so many around the world."

– from the Afterword by **Roger S. Ulrich**, Professor of Architecture, Texas A&M University, and faculty fellow of the Center for Health Systems & Design

"Even Hippocrates understood the power of the arts to promote comfort and healing. Ridenour and Sadler's book is an indispensable compendium of wonderful ideas and resources to assist healthcare organizations in successfully planning and implementing transformative arts programs. It is a must-have!"

– **Susan B. Frampton**, Ph.D., President, Planetree

Transforming the Healthcare Experience through the Arts

Blair L. Sadler
Annette Ridenour

Publisher:
Aesthetics, Inc.
San Diego, California
(619) 683-7500

ISBN 978-0-9842326-0-4
Printed in the United States of America

www.artandhealthcare.com

Contents

Contents

Contents

This book is dedicated to all the artists, caregivers, and leaders whose work already has transformed the healthcare experience for countless patients, families, visitors, and staff – and to all those who will continue to do so in years to come.

Your creativity, commitment, and perseverance honor what it means to be fully alive and responsive to the needs of others. This book, inspired by your achievements and your aspirations, is our gesture of appreciation to you.

Annette Ridenour

Preface

Anita Boles, Executive Director, Society for the Arts in Healthcare

Twenty years ago, twelve pioneers came together to create a new organization, which was first called the Society of Healthcare Arts Administrators and soon became the Society for the Arts in Healthcare. Today, the Society has more than 1,700 individual, student, and organizational members throughout the world.

Credit for that growth can be found in many places: in artists with a passion for helping others at key moments in their lives; in healthcare organizations that honored the essential connection of body, mind, and spirit; in individual nurses, physicians, and other healthcare professionals who initiated art projects in their own spheres of responsibility; in farsighted educators who taught others about the restorative powers of the arts; in nonprofit and government agencies that understood the growing evidence regarding the efficacy of integrative healthcare and supported those who were practicing it; and in the members, staff, and leaders of the Society for the Arts in Healthcare who tirelessly dedicated themselves to supporting all those efforts and spreading the word about them.

And yet there is more, the "more" that Don Berwick and Lee Kaiser so eloquently describe in this book. Throughout recorded history, we see evidence that pictures, stories, dances, music, and drama have been central to healing rituals. Today's renewed focus on humanistic care is leading to resurgence in the knowledge and practice of incorporating the arts into healthcare services. The growth of the Society for the Arts in Healthcare is not simply the growth of an organization, it is the growth of a renewed understanding of what it means — what it feels like; how much it matters — to be fully human at all the moments of our lives. In the poignant *"Dragonflies of Hope"* story in this book, a hospice director says, "Our belief is that we can put life into days, not days into life." Ultimately, that is all any of us can hope for—more life in all the days we have.

Annette Ridenour and Blair Sadler have championed our cause for a long time. They also recognized the importance of promoting the value of arts in healthcare to those who might need some convincing, so they partnered with the Society to create the Blair L. Sadler International Healing Arts Competition. This ground-breaking competition spurred the gathering of hard evidence about the efficacy of the arts in healthcare and inspired everyone, from experienced artists and healthcare practitioners to students just beginning their careers, to include the measurement of outcomes as an integral part of arts in healthcare programs.

The impact of the Sadler Awards in that regard can be seen throughout this book, and in the Society's 2009 *State of the Field* report, which is cited often within it: There now exists a steadily growing body of scientific evidence sufficient to convince even the most skeptical that what we know in our hearts and need in our souls can be confirmed with our heads. This remarkable and inspiring book represents the culmination of our partnership with Blair and Annette.

The Society for the Arts in Healthcare is proud to represent all those who understand and believe in what this book so powerfully communicates; we are proud of our contribution to what the Sadler Awards have helped bring about; and we are proud of every single instance when an artist and a healthcare provider have joined together to ease pain, add joy, raise hope, and speed healing. This book will certainly advance the arts in healthcare with its examples of excellence in the field, and assuredly add more life to everyone's days.

Foreword

Donald M. Berwick, M.D.
President and CEO, Institute for Healthcare Improvement

The teacher and consultant, Jean Houston, has a little exercise that she uses with her audiences. "What do you want?" she asks, and then she gives them a few minutes to think about their answers and discuss them with a neighbor.

But, she's not done. A second question follows: "What do you *really* want?" And, again a moment follows for reflection and conversation.

And then, she asks, "What do you *really, really* want?" The time for private reflection is a little longer, before the next conversation starts.

When I first heard about that exercise, I tried it on myself. To my surprise, by the third question I was quietly in tears, in a moment of profound joy. I was thinking about my children, my wife, and everything I love in my life. I was thinking about my favorite day of the year, Thanksgiving, when we are all together. What I really, really want is Thanksgiving Day.

Since then, I have tried Jean Houston's questions with healthcare audiences, especially those who have asked me to talk about one of my favorite topics, "patient-centered care."

"With respect to your health and your healthcare," I ask them, "what do you want?" They buzz happily in conversations about "quality of care" and "responsiveness" and "safety" and such. It's an easy moment for conversation.

"What do you *really* want?" The buzzing softens then, and I watch faces get serious, contemplative, curious. They seem to be reaching deeper. "I want my pain to go away." "I want comfort and dignity." "I want the company of my loved ones." "I want to suffer less."

"And, with respect to your health and healthcare, what do you *really, really* want?" Now, the silence lasts a lot longer. Some wipe their eyes. They all look serious, lost in thought. The conversations start slowly, hesitantly and with a hush, and many look downward, as if praying. They, too, are now thinking, I suspect, about their families and the mountains they love to hike in and their music and the evening sky and the peaceful places they go to when they can. They are thinking, "I really, really want Thanksgiving." "I really, really want to stand for a whole hour, just me, in person, in silence, in front of the original of Van Gogh's *Starry Night*, just one more time."

Because of its ancient roots and its technical mystery, healthcare awes us, as a throbbing machine or a giant dam might – as the actual spear of Alexander or the actual pen of Shakespeare might. In awe, we give it power and control – healthcare gets to tell us what to do, how to act, where we may go, and where not. It creates cathedrals, the spaces for its own work, the most majestic of which are hospitals, in which even the most confident among us falls silent and follows the rules. The doctors and nurses who line up with me at the movie theater do no such thing in the hospital; they have their own sacred places there, and, when a patient, I may not enter them. The inspiring mission of healthcare becomes encased in this majesty, its priests wear uniforms, and the experience of care, more and more, becomes disconnected from our lives and selves. Technocracy wins, and souls take second place.

Dig deep. Healthcare is not an end; it is a means. In and of itself, it is of no value whatsoever. For what reason does this great machine throb? Why does this dam stop the river? What war was Alexander fighting and for whom? Shakespeare's pen is just a pen, except for what he wrote, and for what he wrote does for us.

Dig deep. With respect to your health and healthcare, what do you *really, really* want? "Pills?" I doubt it. "Cure?" Actually, not. "Comfort and zest?" Closer, but that's not quite it, either. With time and encouragement, I daresay, most of us would probably get to more or less the same type of answer once the stakes were "really, really." Most of us, I daresay, would name what matters to us in our hearts, whatever that be. I name my family and those I love. You may name the joy of craftsmanship, the beauty of nature, or the love of adventure.

"Joy," "beauty," "love" – do these words really belong to the notion of "quality" in healthcare? Are they not naïve – too far from the cold, hard facts of technology and the scientific foundations of our battle against disease and for health? That, of course, would be the likely criticism of a plea, such as this book makes, to re-unite art and healthcare. It would likely feel as if Blair Sadler and Annette Ridenour are more about the icing than the cake. "Isn't that cute?" the tolerant critics would say. "Maybe someday we should think a bit about art in healthcare, after the real work is done."

But, what Sadler and Ridenour offer here seems to me much more profound. I don't think they are writing about attaching something to the outskirts of care; I think they may be reminding us of first principles – the meaning and purpose of care, itself. They may be reminding us of what we "really, really" want when, in our pain and fear, we reach to the professions and their tools to help us, and, equally important, reminding us of what the professionals, themselves, "really, really" want to offer, through their skill and will, to the people who depend on them. Maybe, just maybe, a new idea gestates in this lovely book: not that art can serve healthcare, but that healthcare can serve art.

What would change if all the care we sought to give and all the tools and time and spaces we used to give it remained continually connected to the deeper purposes, not of healthcare, but of the lives that healthcare seeks to nurture and extend? Suppose healthcare, mindfully, existed precisely to offer us all what we really, really want? How would that change our dialogue with patients, families, and communities? How would that guide us to different investments, new priorities, and altered choices? How would we train our young then, and what would we want to know about our patients?

The premise in this book, I propose, is less that art counts in healthcare than that souls count in healthcare. That there appears to be evidence that enriching healthcare spaces and times with painting, dance, music, and storytelling seems to help healing speed up and pain to tone down. That is encouraging, and may provide a bridging rationale for what these authors hope for. But, frankly, for me, I don't know how much more evidence I need to make me sure that, when I see my doctor, or, as a doctor, when I see my patient, our shared aim can and ought to take us leagues beyond the tools and devices that both connect and separate us. I don't know that I need much more evidence that care can and ought to bring the helper and the helped closer, ever closer, to a sense of our shared humanness. I love Brahms; maybe my doctor does, too.

The authors write, "The days of depersonalized, frightening, noisy, and confusing care environments are numbered. Today's foresighted healthcare leaders are freed to honor the full panoply of human aspiration, as expressed through the arts, within their institutions' activities and their physical designs." After reading this deeply important book, you may join me in hoping so.

Foreword

Leland R. Kaiser, Ph.D.
Health Futurist

As you open this book you will begin a remarkable journey through a frontier area of healthcare, destined to become one of the most significant future advances in patient health and well-being.

I have enjoyed the great privilege of working with both of the authors – Blair Sadler and Annette Ridenour. I hold them in high regard. Not only are they highly talented, they are also fearless pioneers in improving patient care experiences through the incorporation of arts projects and programs in healthcare environments. In this book they give us many examples of the healing potentials of good environmental design.

A well-designed patient habitat should be considered an important therapeutic tool and part of our medical armamentarium. A healing environment supplements, complements and in many cases extends the effectiveness of surgical interventions and medications. In some cases, the environment, in and of itself, becomes a powerful therapeutic agent with measurable treatment outcomes. A good general design principle to remember is that sick environments make patients sicker and healthy environments make patients healthier.

We used to think of healthcare facilities as spaces that held things – empty containers if you will. Now, we know the spaces themselves make powerful statements about how we view our patients and what we expect from them. Well-designed spaces provide opportunities for inspiration, participation, regeneration, and personal fulfillment. They provide a context for everything else we do for our patients. Spaces are not passive containers. They are active radiators. They project emotional, mental, and spiritual content. They stimulate response and provide a medium for patient transformation that goes well beyond treatment of a disease or disability. Well-designed patient spaces evoke health potentials and promote the well-being of staff members, patients, family members, and even visitors.

All of us are the sum total of our life experience. Our experiences take place in environments. A design for an environment is therefore a design for human consciousness. We should think of patient care spaces as opportunities to provide valuable new experiences that alter patient awareness in health-giving ways. Healing spaces are experiential spaces and can be designed with this intent. As the patient interacts with these spaces, the patient is transformed.

The good news is, you don't have to start from scratch in learning about experiential design. This book is chock full of examples of effective arts programs in a variety of healthcare settings. It goes beyond theory and concept. It gives us the names and locations of destination facilities and the important people connected with them. The authors tell us who we should know and where we should go. They take us far beyond a typical academic treatise on healthcare design. They provide us with a rich resource manual containing the current state of the art in experiential habitat design. They have given us a great menu for site visits by our physicians, trustees, and administrators.

This book is a valuable resource manual you will often consult. I consider it essential for anyone building a new healthcare facility or remodeling an existing facility.

Arts projects and programs are not architectural add-ons or fringe niceties. They are an essential part of core design and dramatically affect patient care outcomes. This book makes a major contribution to the developing literature on evidence-based environmental design. In addition, it is fun to read and is beautifully illustrated.

Hats off to Blair Sadler and Annette Ridenour! They have given us a work that is destined to become a classic in the literature of healthcare.

Acknowledgments

We appreciate the dedication, hard work, and guidance of the jury committee members who met with us for three days each year over the seven years of the Sadler Awards program. They tirelessly reviewed and ranked each of the many applications to the competition as they also helped us build and refine the program each year. A special thanks to Cam Busch, Lillian Fitzgerald, Leah Goodwin, Judy Rollins, Larry Scott, and Naj Wykoff for their contributions to this important work.

Some of the information for chapter two was provided by Dr. Judy Rollins, who is widely recognized as a leader in the field of research methodology related to healthcare and the arts.

Aesthetics staff members Peggy McCartney and Jan Carpenter Tucker deserve special recognition. Peggy was the creative force behind the design and layout of the book. Jan served diligently for several years as liaison with the many artists who applied for and won awards, and helped organize their materials for inclusion.

The heart and soul of the book are found in the work of the artists themselves and in the partnerships they forged with remarkable healthcare and community organizations. Whether they work as painters, musicians, dancers, writers, or film-makers, the artists are true pioneers in creativity and compassion. The stories of their work that we present here are vivid examples of how the arts can help heal people, organizations, and communities.

We are grateful to the Society for the Arts in Healthcare, which partnered with us in the Sadler Awards program from the beginning. The program was supported by three different executive directors of the Society for the Arts in Healthcare — Suzy Brenner, Gay Hanna, and Anita Boles — and many members the Society's board of directors were steadfast supporters as well.

This book has been a truly collaborative effort. Jerry de Jaager has been our tireless editor for over two years. His belief in the importance of this effort has made him an important partner in the writing of this book. As one not directly involved in healthcare and the arts, he provided a vitally important perspective. Without his dedication and talent, this book would not have been possible.

Finally, we would like to acknowledge our spouses, Georgia Robins Sadler and Roger Hill, whose important advice and moral support sustained us throughout this project.

Part I

The Vital Role of the Arts in Healthcare

"The Journey"
Artist: Michele Angelo Petrone
© MAP Foundation

"We were made to enjoy music, to enjoy beautiful sunsets, to enjoy looking at the billows of the sea and to enjoy looking at a rose that is bedecked with dew…. Human beings are actually created for the transcendent, for the sublime, for the beautiful, for the truthful…and all of us are given the task of trying to make the world a little more hospitable to these beautiful things."

– Desmond Tutu

"Every day, low-cost, high-impact arts programs are calming, soothing, uplifting, and restoring patients – reducing their suffering, empowering them to move forward, lifting the quality of their days, giving them solace, and supporting those who love them, care for them, and care about them.

But every day is not the same as everywhere. According to recent research, more than half of American hospitals have no arts programs at all. Many of the finest, most effective arts interventions are used in only a handful of places, even though they could be applicable virtually everywhere."

– page 27

Healthcare Leadership and Healing Arts Programs

Arts-based programs and projects help healthcare leaders succeed in fulfilling crucial responsibilities that include patient satisfaction, safety, quality, and implementing evidence-based design principles.

Rady Children's Hospital, San Diego, California
Artist: Dennis Smith

More than ever before, healthcare executives today can apply all the resources available to them to produce superb results in cost-effective ways. This book contains 36 examples of arts projects and programs that positively affect important healthcare outcomes, generally for little cost. Created by a wide range of artists – including musicians, writers, dancers, painters, and film-makers – and implemented within caring healthcare institutions, the projects decrease pain, combat anxiety, stress, and depression, and raise spirits. They beautify the institution and humanize the way it is experienced. They raise staff morale, increase community involvement, give patients greater capacity to fight their illnesses, and strengthen families' ability to care for loved ones.

For all those reasons and many more, healthcare arts projects and programs can increase the satisfaction of patients, families, and visitors. Moreover, some save money and most are easy to implement. Arts applications also contribute to healthcare executives' important task of finding cost-effective ways to treat, honor, and satisfy their organizations' patients and those who care for them and about them.

The initial costs of designing and implementing arts programs can often be obtained through special grants that are either renewed or expanded as the programs demonstrate their continued value. That continuation or expansion often occurs through the acquisition of private and foundation money from new sources. At the same time, more organizations are recognizing the value of arts programs and funding them internally: a recent survey reported that in 2004, 40 percent cited their organization's operating budget as a source of funding for arts programs; in 2007, that percentage had risen to 56.[1]

FOUR IMPORTANT TRENDS

In the current healthcare environment, and into the foreseeable future, four general trends are creating particular pressures on healthcare executives to accomplish more. Those trends are as follows: the mandatory collection and reporting of patient satisfaction information; the healthcare quality/safety revolution; the growing influence of evidence-based design; and the increasing impact of the "baby boom" generation.

Within each of those trends, arts applications can substantially improve a healthcare organization's performance.

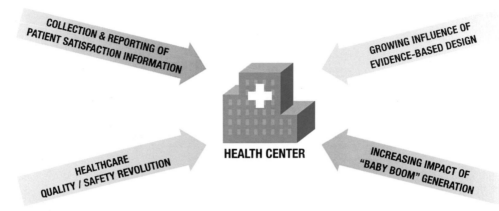

COLLECTION & REPORTING OF PATIENT SATISFACTION INFORMATION

GROWING INFLUENCE OF EVIDENCE-BASED DESIGN

HEALTH CENTER

HEALTHCARE QUALITY / SAFETY REVOLUTION

INCREASING IMPACT OF "BABY BOOM" GENERATION

Quantifying and Reporting Patient Satisfaction

The Consumer Assessment of Healthcare Providers and Systems Hospital Survey, known as Hospital CAHPS or HCAHPS, went into effect on October 1, 2008. This mandatory survey collects information from Medicare patients to facilitate hospital-by-hospital comparisons of patient satisfaction and increase institutional accountability. Survey results are published in easy-to-use online and printed formats, permitting, for example, comparisons among hospitals within a certain number of miles from a potential patient's home.

Rady Children's Hospital

Patient satisfaction questionnaires have been used for many years, but they have always been voluntary, there has been no common format among them, and hospitals were not required to release the results to the public. Until now, patients, families, and payers have had no place to obtain comparable patient-satisfaction information. Although HCAHPS was initially limited to Medicare patients, its expansion to other patients is virtually assured; in fact, Medicaid programs in several states are now adopting it or variations of it, and some commercial payers are using it as well. Scores are already being publicized by individual hospitals to demonstrate their success at satisfying patients.

The eighteen substantive questions within HCAHPS include both general indicators of satisfaction – "Using any number from 0 to 10, where 0 is the worst hospital possible and 10 is the best hospital possible, what number would you use to rate this hospital during your stay?" – and more specific factors – "During this hospital stay, how often did the hospital staff do everything they could to help you with your pain?" It is noteworthy that patients are not asked in these questions and others to accept the environment and their treatment as they are provided to them, but to imagine the best environment and treatment they could have received – the "best hospital possible" and caregivers who "do everything they could."

Rady Children's Hospital
Artist: T.J. Dixon

Patients and their families who are deciding which hospital and physician to use will likely begin to place substantial weight on the last of the substantive questions: "Would you recommend this hospital to your friends and family?"

As consumers increasingly use HCAHPS comparisons to evaluate hospitals and make informed choices about where they will receive care, wise executives will increasingly utilize the low-cost, high-impact potential of arts applications to help improve patient satisfaction scores. In doing so, they will help differentiate themselves from their competitors. Improved reputation scores and greater patient volume should result.

The model put forth by Planetree, for example, focusing on the healing of mind, body, and spirit and including an active arts component, has yielded superior HCAHPS scores. As a group, hospitals that have comprehensively implemented the Planetree model exceed the national benchmarks in all ten of the publicly-reported HCAHPS categories, with the most significant differences appearing on the questions related to overall rating of the hospital and willingness to recommend it to others.[2]

The Healthcare Safety/Quality Revolution

The healthcare safety/quality revolution was catalyzed by two landmark Institute of Medicine reports published at the beginning of this decade, *To Err is Human*[3] and *Crossing the Quality Chasm*.[4] They documented the thousands of unnecessary deaths that were occurring in American hospitals every year because of system failures, and set forth a series of recommendations for improvement. The movement has been further stimulated by the nonprofit Institute for Healthcare Improvement in collaboration with many others.[5]

Two major safety/quality campaigns, the 100,000 Lives Campaign and the Protecting 5 Million Lives from Harm Campaign, have enrolled over four thousand American hospitals representing more than 80 percent of the country's acute-care beds. The quality revolution is demonstrating that better outcomes occur when healthcare institutions pay close attention to the six dimensions of excellence identified by the Institute of Medicine. Those dimensions are effectiveness, safety, patient-centeredness, efficiency, timeliness, and equity. As the projects described in this book show, arts applications can make an important difference, at low cost, within each of those six critical dimensions.

Art Programs Support the Institute of Medicine's Six Domains of Quality

The arts are demonstrating their *effectiveness* as healing modalities, even in comparison to some accepted medical practices. They are increasing *safety* by eliminating or reducing the use of anesthesia and pharmaceutical drugs. They are *patient-centered*, in part because their very purpose for existing is to meet individual patient needs, and in part because they can utilize the patient's own resources for healing rather than something extraneous to the patient.

Regarding *efficiency*, some arts applications can reduce the need for expensive medical personnel and allow procedures to be completed more quickly. They also can make some treatment more expeditious because patients experiencing less pain and less distress are easier to talk to and their complaints can be more quickly addressed.

As for *timeliness*, the Institute of Medicine says "the system should anticipate patient needs, rather than simply reacting to events." Arts strategies such as those discussed in this book – for example, providing positive distractions to children in an emergency room or offering an effective anti-depression modality to family caregivers before they come to require medical attention for depression – help make those medical

Children waiting to be seen in a hospital emergency room participate in an *Art While You Wait* project.
Photo by Kyle McDonald

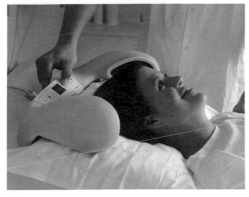
A patient listens to specially-designed music by *MusiCure*.
Photo by Björn Wennerwald

services anticipatory rather than reactive in a way that is consistent with the timelines criterion.

The arts are also remarkably *equitable*. Carefully selected music and art can communicate to persons regardless of their cultural heritage or religious affiliation, education or income levels, age, race, or gender. The arts have the advantage of being, to a large extent, "universal languages." The Art While You Wait program described on page 69, for example, now serves children from diverse backgrounds in a wide range of communities. The calming music created by MusiCure (page 39), which was recorded in Denmark, is being used throughout the world.

Carefully chosen art and music interventions provide any healthcare organization with low-cost opportunities to improve performance within all six key dimensions of quality.

The Growth of Evidence-Based Design

Evidence-based design is the deliberate attempt to base building decisions on the evidence available, achieve the best possible outcomes for patients, families, and staff, and improve the utilization of resources.[6] And 2008 was a watershed year for the understanding of evidence-based design. A multidisciplinary team that conducted an exhaustive review of the world's evidence-based design literature reported in *Health Environments Research & Design Journal*, "It is now widely recognized that well designed physical settings play an important role in making hospitals less risky and stressful, promoting more healing for patients, and providing better places for staff to work."[7]

A second comprehensive review, titled *Evidence for Innovation* and focused on the pediatric evidence-based design literature, was also published in 2008. The authors concluded: "[T]he physical environment of pediatric settings impacts clinical, developmental, psychosocial, and safety outcomes among patients and families. The physical

Rady Children's Hospital
Artist: Mario Uribe

environment is a key component of providing patient and family centered care and increasing safety and overall quality of care in pediatric settings."[8]

Bedside Harp founder Edie Elkan plays for a patient. *Photo property of Bedside Harp*

In many situations, evidence-based design research has enabled executives and designers to replace their best-informed intuitive assessments of what environmental factors would be best for patients with solid experimental findings. For example, much of the research on design and layout and choices of materials and equipment has been driven by the goal of reducing hospital-acquired infections.[9] There is also an increasing body of evidence upon which decisions about the appropriateness of art imagery can be based, as well as substantive research showing how music, art-making, and performance can reduce pain and stress related to the healthcare experience. As one 2009 study notes, "[P]aralleling the evidence-based medicine movement in the larger healthcare field, quantitative research in arts in healthcare is being carried out in the U.S. and throughout the world."[10]

Rady Children's Hospital
Artists: Mary Lynn Dominguez and Ellen Phillips

Writing in *The Lancet* in 2001, one author predicted, "Although the premise that the physical environment affects well-being reflects common sense, evidence-based design is poised to emulate evidence-based medicine as a central tenet for healthcare in the twenty-first century."[11] Similarly, arts applications reflect a common sense of their own – that patients and staff are generally healthier and happier in environments that honor the inherent human desire for beauty, peace, and inspiration – and such applications can be expected to increasingly find a place in healthcare delivery.

The Growing Impact of the Baby Boomers

The seventy-eight million members of the baby boom generation are placing unprecedented demands on the healthcare system, and will continue to do so into the foreseeable future. Announcing a 2008 report by a committee of the Institute of Medicine, committee chair John W. Rowe of Columbia University's Mailman School of Public Health echoed what many others have observed: "We face an impending crisis as the growing number of older patients, who are

Rady Children's Hospital
Artists: Mary Lynn Dominguez and Jess Dominguez

living longer with more complex health needs, increasingly outpaces the number of healthcare providers with the knowledge and skills to care for them capably."[12]

Additionally, the baby boomers have led a shift in attitudes toward healthcare, increasingly seeing themselves not as "patients" but as "consumers" of healthcare, who, as one author has stated, "expect to receive full information, demand to participate in healthcare decisions that directly affect them, and insist that the healthcare they receive be of the highest possible quality."[13]

"Quality" for these consumers includes all aspects of the healthcare experience, not just the quality of the interaction with a direct medical service provider. Ambiance, ease of finding one's way, convenience of scheduling, and a host of other environmental and service-related characteristics affect the baby boomers' perception of the quality of care they have received. This is the generation that embraced alternative and complementary forms of healthcare, which often are practiced in warm and appealing environments staffed by warm and caring people. Many baby boomers feel entitled to expect similar settings for all their healthcare services.

As informed consumers with high aspirations, this group can be expected to harshly evaluate facilities that do not meet those aspirations and to select facilities that seem to meet them better, even if some inconvenience, such as additional travel time, is involved. For reasons described above, we believe that healthcare leaders who incorporate the arts and arts programs into their facilities are more likely to win favor with this large and growing demographic group.

Conclusion

The American healthcare-delivery system faces great changes. In an attempt to manage what are widely viewed as out-of-control costs and to make access to care more equitable, some form of systemic reform seems likely. Whatever direction that reform eventually takes, healthcare executives will want to address the four trends described here: mandatory patient satisfaction measures; the safety/quality revolution; the growth of evidence-based design; and the growing impact of the baby boomer generation. As suggested above

Rady Children's Hospital
Artists: Mary Lynn Dominguez and Ellen Phillips

and demonstrated throughout this book, visual, performing, and participatory art projects can be effective strategic tools for helping to address those four trends. Moreover, arts applications also address the most basic responsibilities of healthcare providers, such as managing pain, expediting recovery, and reinforcing the healing willpower of patients and their families.

The days of depersonalized, frightening, noisy, and confusing care environments are numbered. Research, experience, and common sense demonstrate that the arts are appropriate, effective, and cost-efficient strategies. The relatively low cost of arts programs can often be funded by philanthropic sources in the arts community that do not compete with other fundraising initiatives. Today's foresighted healthcare leaders are freed to honor the full panoply of human aspiration, as expressed through the arts, within their institutions' activities and their physical designs. Effectively incorporating those qualities into the culture and fabric of the organization will benefit patients and their loved ones, caregivers, the larger community, and the bottom line.

NIH on the Health Benefits of the Arts

"[S]cientists are finding that the arts can benefit both your mental and physical health. Current research is following a number of paths. Some scientists measure the natural substances your body produces when you're listening to music or otherwise exposed to the arts. Others look at what happens when you are active in the creative process. Researchers are now investigating how the arts can help us recover from disease, injury, and psychological trauma. Many scientists agree that the arts can help reduce stress and anxiety, improve well-being, and enhance the way we fight infection."

– National Institutes of Health[14]

1. State of the Field Committee. *State of the Field: Arts in Healthcare 2009*. (Washington, DC: Society for the Arts in Healthcare, 2009)

2. Personal communication from Dr. Susan Frampton, President, Planetree (August 6, 2009).

3. Committee on Quality of Healthcare in America, Institute of Medicine. *To Err is Human: Building A Safer Health System*. (Washington, D.C.: National Academies Press, 2000)

4. Committee on Quality of Healthcare in America, Institute of Medicine. *Crossing the Quality Chasm: Building A New Health System for the 21st Century*. (Washington, D.C.: National Academies Press, 2001)

5. See Sadler, Blair. "To the Class of 2005: Will You Be Ready for the Quality Revolution?" *Joint Commission Journal on Quality and Patient Safety*, 32(1), 51-55 (2006)

6. See Sadler, Blair. "The Compelling Business Case for Building Optimal Healing Environments." Presentation at the Health Environment Facilities Management Association Annual Conference. (London, 2009)

7. Ulrich, R. S., Zimring, C. M., Zhu, X., et al. "A Review of the Research Literature on Evidence-Based Health-care Design." *Health Environments Research & Design*, 1(3): 63 (2008)

8. National Association of Children's Hospitals and Related Institutions. *Evidence for Innovation: Transforming Children's Health through the Physical Environment* (Alexandria, VA: NACHRI, 2008)

9. Sadler, B., Joseph, A., Keller, A., and Rostenberg, B. "Using Evidence-Based Environmental Design to Enhance Safety and Quality." *IHI Innovation Series White Paper*. (Cambridge, MA: Institute for Healthcare Improvement, 2009)

10. State of the Field Committee. *State of the Field: Arts in Healthcare 2009*. (Washington, DC: Society for the Arts in Healthcare, 2009)

11. Martin, Colin. "Putting Patients First: Integrating Hospital Design and Care." *The Lancet* 2000; 356: 9228 518

12. Committee on the Future Health Care Workforce for Older Americans, Institute of Medicine. *Retooling for an Aging America: Building the Healthcare Workforce*. (Washington, D.C.: National Academies Press, 2008)

13. Thomas, Richard. *Health Communication*. (New York: Springer, 2005)

14. National Institutes of Health. "More Than A Feeling: How the Arts Affect Your Health." *NIH News in Health* (June, 2008)

"Within a relatively short period of time, the arts have demonstrated their effectiveness at improving the physical, emotional, and psychological well-being of patients, visitors, and staff."

– page 20

The Healing Intersection between the Arts and Healthcare

AtlantiCare Regional Medical Center,
Center for Childbirth, Pomona, New Jersey
Artist: Jonathan Darmon

When caring artists and compassionate healthcare organizations join forces, the results cannot just be felt, they can be measured.

The projects and programs in this book reflect the intersection of an artist or team of artists looking for a way to bring more compassion, less suffering, and more joy into the healthcare experience, and a healthcare organization committed to the same goals.

With just a few exceptions, it has only been in the past few decades that healthcare institutions have purposefully employed the arts to affect patients' well-being and improve the healthcare experience. According to a study conducted in 2007, about 45 percent of American healthcare organizations have arts programs serving patients, visitors, and staff.[1]

Facilities with arts programs cited several advantages, including increased patient satisfaction, a more positive healing environment, better physical and emotional recovery, improved community relations, and support for hospital staff.

Of the many kinds of arts programs offered within the healthcare setting, the most common is art hung on the walls of corridors, patient rooms, and other areas. Just over 35 percent of institutions report having a permanent art collection.[2]

Arts performances in public areas, group arts activities, and creative arts therapies lead the next tier of representation in healthcare facilities.

Fewer than 20 percent of those surveyed have artists (musicians, visual artists, and others) visiting patient rooms, and fewer than 10 percent offer arts activities in waiting rooms.

In considering the current and future adoption of arts activities within healthcare, it is valuable to distinguish among arts therapies, arts programming, and visual art (art collections or "art on the walls").

Arts Therapies

An *Arts Access* staff member assists a young patient working on a digital painting.
Photo by Lyn Sanders

Although the history of arts therapies stretches back more than 100 years, such therapies generally began reaching into healthcare in the 1970s and 1980s. Arts therapies use artistic expression as a way to help patients cope with symptoms of pain, stress, and trauma, enhance their cognitive abilities, and increase awareness of themselves and others. Arts therapists are licensed and trained artists who are knowledgeable about human development, psychological theories, clinical practice, and spiritual, multicultural, and artistic traditions, as well as the healing potential of art.

Because arts therapy is a recognized professional discipline and because it has been establishing itself within healthcare for some time, considerable investigation has been conducted into its efficacy. Because that investigation has frequently substantiated that efficacy, institutions have been increasingly willing to adopt arts therapies interventions.

For example, in the case reported on pages 34-37 of this book, careful analysis of the effects of music therapy in one unit of the Cleveland Clinic (the Harry R. Horvitz Center for Palliative Medicine at the Clinic's Taussig Cancer Institute) has led the Clinic to expand music therapy into other units. At Tallahassee Memorial Hospital, music played by a music therapist with children who are anxious about an impending noninvasive medical procedure (such as an echocardiogram or CT scan) has been shown to virtually eliminate the need for pharmaceutical sedation for many of those young patients (see pages 72-75). Now the hospital is applying the methodology of that program in other areas of care, such as the insertion of intravenous lines in children and reducing anxiety in adults and children during MRI scans.

Assessment of the efficacy of arts therapies solidifies and expands the intersection between caring artists and caring institutions.

Arts Programming

Arts programming involves the use of the arts, without a participating therapist, to affect the well-being of patients and others, and to improve the quality of the healthcare experience.

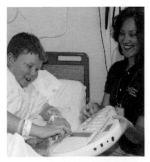

A young patient enjoys a musical interlude through the *Music Rx®* program.

These programs can include art collections (which are discussed as a separate category in the next section), participatory programs, and performance programs. Participatory programs – of which there are many examples in Part II of this book – engage patients and others in activities that include the art-making, writing, and musical activities. Performance programs include non-participatory attendance at events such as musical and theatrical performances.

AtlantiCare Regional Medical Center, City Campus
Artist: Liz Nicklus

Perhaps because arts programming is often provided by volunteer artists and often is funded through grants that do not impinge substantially on institutional budgets, assessments of the impacts of arts programming have been undertaken less often than assessments of arts therapy interventions – usually to meet funders' and institutions' evaluation requirements, rather than as substantial explorations of their healing impact. However, that is changing rapidly as practitioners, institutions, and medical researchers become more aware of the significant healing and restorative powers of arts programming.

At a hospital in Northern Ireland, for example, a three-year project measured the effects of art-making on patients, staff, and others (see pages 30-33). The results were striking: among other things, nearly 50 percent of the participants told researchers that their pain and other symptoms were relieved by their art activities. Over 90 percent said they were more relaxed and that their moods improved.

In Denmark, musicians worked with physicians to record specially-designed healing music, and tested its effects on patients in many settings; again, the results indisputably demonstrated positive changes (see pages 38-41). That music now is being utilized in hospitals and other healthcare institutions around the world.

In a study reported in 2008, a team from Massachusetts General Hospital enabled some critically-ill post-operative patients to listen to Mozart sonatas through headphones. A control group received no music. Those who listened to

Loma Linda University Medical Center,
Loma Linda, California   Artist: Vickie Asp

the music required less sedative medication than the members of the control group, and analysis of blood samples showed that the group of listeners had higher plasma concentrations of beneficial growth hormones and lower levels of the stress hormones interleukin-6 and epinephrine. "The reduction in systemic stress hormone levels was associated with a significantly lower blood pressure and heart rate," the researchers reported.[3]

As impact assessments continue to demonstrate positive outcomes from arts programming, more institutions will invite artists into collaborative ventures to serve their stakeholders.

A Major New Force for Understanding and Change – Neuroaesthetics

The new field of neuroaesthetics – in which brain scans are employed to study neurological reactions to perceived beauty, ugliness, and other aesthetic phenomena – is opening another front. Dr. Semir Zeki of University College London is a leading neuroaesthetics researcher. Here's how one writer described one of Zeki's more intriguing, and potentially pertinent, findings:

> In 2004 [Dr. Zeki] led a neuroimaging study designed to investigate the neural correlates of beauty. Ten participants were shown 300 paintings and asked to classify each of them as beautiful, ugly, or neutral.... The participants were then shown the paintings again while lying in a scanner. "Beautiful" paintings elicited increased activity in the orbito-frontal cortex, which is involved in emotion and reward. Interestingly, the "uglier" a painting, the greater the motor cortex activity, as if the brain was preparing to escape.[4]

The brain's escape response entails the release of stress hormones, increases in pulse and heart rates, and many other unhealthy reactions, suggesting that art may have a physical effect on patients.

Art Collections

Glendale Adventist Medical Center,
Glendale, California
Artist: Ken Goldman

As mentioned earlier, arts programming also includes art collections. Nowhere is perceived beauty more pertinent to healthcare administrators than in this area. Although few reliable studies exist, a 1991 study by Roger Ulrich, a pioneer of evidence-based design research, is a notable exception. Ulrich's research in a Swedish hospital demonstrated that intensive care patients following heart surgery viewing pictures of a landscape scene with trees and water reported less anxiety and stress, and needed less pain medication, than those in control groups without any pictures and those with pictures depicting abstract imagery.[5]

Most of the investigations in the visual arts that have followed Ulrich's pioneering research have been in the form of "preference studies," in which individuals are asked what artwork they like and what artwork they don't like. In general, and across many different populations, they show a preference for landscapes over other depictions. Preference studies can be useful, but it is likely that more substantive research, including neuroaesthetics research, will supplant them in the future.

Kaiser Permanente, San Marcos, California
Artist: Ed Wordell

Because there have been practically no objective criteria, beyond the general preference for landscapes, for the selection and utilization of artworks in healthcare, leaders, teams, and others have often made artwork selections based on their own intuitive sense of what patients and visitors would prefer. Given the strong positive and negative effects of art on individuals, and the variability of individuals' likes and dislikes, two implications seem clear. First, experienced experts with knowledge of existing and emerging research findings have much to add to the important process of selecting artworks for maximum positive impact. Second, variability in individual preferences should be accommodated as much as possible – for example, by allowing patients to select the art that hangs in their rooms or in their areas of their rooms. Providing patient choice is important.

Visual Art as a Strategic Tool for Executives – A Case Study

In some forward-looking facilities, the art collection has been seen as a way to both beautify the environment and accomplish broader goals. Lori Herndon, president and CEO of AtlantiCare Regional Medical Center in New Jersey, has written:

> The more we have accepted the arts, and artists, at AtlantiCare, the more benefits we have gained. Those benefits include high levels of patient and staff satisfaction, praise from the community and the media, and a distinctive branding advantage. They also include the infusion of a new and different, but very positive, kind of energy into the way we approach and make decisions.[6]

AtlantiCare created a true, collaborative intersection between artists and the institution. To accomplish that, AtlantiCare used a carefully structured internal process to identify desired outcomes for its visual-art program, and then further defined its goals through a strategic process guided by a community-based arts committee. The resulting principles, policies, and procedures led to a major collection of regional artists' work. (The full process used by AtlantiCare was similar to the one described in chapter 10.)

AtlantiCare Regional Medical Center, City Campus
Artists: Deborah Sachs and Marilyn Keating

Outcomes were measured over two years, assessing patient, staff, and visitor reaction to the new art. Increasingly positive responses demonstrated that the art was highly effective in supporting key goals of the institution, and that its impact was sustained. Here are some sample results from the survey:

How much the artwork lowered the stress levels of patients and visitors:

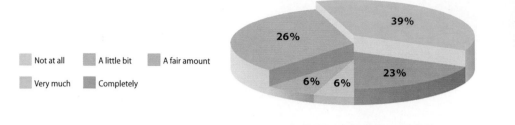

Not at all A little bit A fair amount Very much Completely

39% 26% 23% 6% 6%

Patients' and visitors' views of the importance of having all of the artists be from the community:

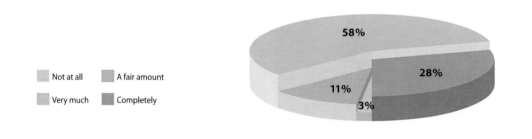

Not at all A fair amount Very much Completely

58% 28% 11% 3%

How much the artwork influenced patients' and visitors' overall experience at AtlantiCare:

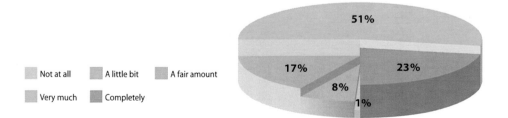

Not at all A little bit A fair amount Very much Completely

51% 23% 17% 8% 1%

With this information, AtlantiCare senior leadership decided to expand the program to all its facilities, including furnishing a new seven-story patient tower with over 900 artworks.

The Artist-Administrator Interface and the Origins of This Book

This book itself arises from a longstanding collaboration between its co-authors: a hospital leader, Blair Sadler, and an artist/designer with a healthcare arts consulting firm, Annette Ridenour.

Rady Children's Hospital
Artists: Mary Lynn Dominguez and Ellen Phillips

In 1990, when Blair was president and CEO of Children's Hospital San Diego (subsequently renamed Rady Children's Hospital), Annette's firm, Aesthetics, Inc., was retained to assist with a visual arts program. Since then, we have collaborated on many projects, all aimed at using the latest evidence to create an environment that is healing, soothing, and inspiring for children, their parents, and everyone else who visits or works there.

Currently, Rady Children's has over 300 works of visual art, English- and Spanish-speaking storytellers, numerous musicians, visual artists in residence, a therapeutic harp program, and several galleries featuring changing displays of community and children's art. The hospital has been a leader in the use of healing gardens, and several have been created for patients and their families. Each involved commissioning many

Sharp Memorial Hospital and Rady Children's MRI Center, San Diego, California
Artist: Tom Fagan

artists and designers to transform lackluster courtyards into whimsical outdoor retreats. These peaceful sanctuaries provide quiet respite for patients, families, and staff, promoting health and well-being for all who visit.

Rady Children's Hospital
Artist: Alber De Motteis

The overall impact of the gardens and the campus was powerfully described in 2004 by Gina Wright, the garden editor and established writer for *Decor & Style* magazine. She wrote, "I know I shall never get Children's Hospital out of my system. I have been back several times – it is a wonderful and inspiring place to visit even if one does not have a particular reason to be there."[7]

The Sadler Awards

In 2000, we realized the critical importance of documenting and highlighting the place of the arts within healthcare and encouraging artists and institutions to study the impacts of their creative work. That realization led to the creation of the Blair L. Sadler International Healing Arts Competition, which has recognized individuals and teams for exemplary healthcare arts projects. It was co-designed and led by

A young patient and her mother read *Oodles of Doodles*, created by *Art with Heart*. Photo by Richard Brown

Blair and Annette and underwritten by Blair in partnership with the Society for the Arts in Healthcare (the Society). Each year a jury of reviewers with significant experience in the arts and healthcare – often including members of the Society's board of directors – has evaluated the applications and selected the winners.

Until the awards competition was created, there was little professional recognition for the contribution of the arts in healthcare, and no structured way of drawing attention to the kinds of programs that were transforming the healthcare experience.

An Alzheimer's patient and her granddaughter play the board game *Making Memories Together*.

Part II of this book features case studies selected from award-winning entries to that competition. Those earning first place designations demonstrated quantified results of the impact of their project or program through an evaluative study. Honorable mention recognition was given to exemplary projects lacking solid outcome studies.

In a third category, for students, the design of an outcome study – if not its implementation – was required. The student category was intended to inspire schools of art, medicine, and nursing to develop curricula incorporating the arts as an effective catalyst in the healing process.[8]

Conclusion

Within a relatively short period of time, the arts have demonstrated their effectiveness at improving the physical, emotional, and psychological well-being of patients, visitors, and staff. In addition to those specific benefits, arts therapies, arts programming, and visual arts elevate caring and compassion to the forefront of the healthcare experience. Continuing investigation of the effects of the arts is likely to further validate the effectiveness of arts applications as a resource for healthcare leaders and further expand this important intersection between healthcare and the arts.

THE ARTS AND HEALING OUTCOMES: SOME INVESTIGATIVE FINDINGS

In addition to the studies mentioned in this chapter, other research and evaluation studies have shown how the arts can produce positive outcomes. Some of those studies are briefly described here.

For Inpatients

Patients on a trauma and orthopedics ward who were exposed to visual arts and live music had shorter stays and needed significantly less pain relief than patients in a control group. [Staricoff, R. L., Duncan, J., Wright, M., Loppert, S., and Scott, J. "A Study of The Effects of Visual and Performing Arts in Healthcare." *Hospital Development* (June, 2001)]

Individuals with cancer who participated in a one-hour art therapy session reported statistically significant reduction in eight of nine symptoms common to adult cancer inpatients – pain, tiredness, depression, anxiety, drowsiness, appetite, well-being, and breathlessness. [Nainis, N., Paice, J., Ratner, J., Wirth, J., Lai, J., and Shott, S. "Relieving Symptoms in Cancer: Innovative Use of Art Therapy." *Journal of Pain and Symptom Management,* 31(2), 162–169 (2006)]

Patients hospitalized for high-dose therapy with stem cell transplantation who participated in a music therapy group scored 28 percent lower on the combined Anxiety/Depression scale and 37 percent lower on the total mood disturbance score compared to controls without music therapy. [Cassileth, B., Vickers, A., and Magill, L. "Music Therapy for Mood Disturbance During Hospitalization for Autologous Stem Cell Transplantation: A Randomized Controlled Trial." *Cancer,* 98(12), 2723–2729 (2003)]

Musical instruments used in musical therapy
Photo by Judy Nguyen Engel

Four or more one-hour water-painting sessions reduced depression and fatigue in cancer patients, compared to two or fewer sessions. [Bar-Sela, G., Atid, L., Dans, S., Gabay, N., and Epelbaum, P. "Art Therapy Reduced Depression and Improved Fatigue Levels in Cancer Patients on Chemotherapy."*Psychooncology,* 16, 980–984 (2007)]

Quality of life improved and increased over time for adults in hospice care receiving music therapy; individuals in the control group experienced a lower quality of life and their quality of life decreased over time. [Hilliard, R. "The Effects of Music Therapy on the Quality and Length of Life of People Diagnosed with Terminal Cancer." *Journal of Music Therapy,* 40, 113–137 (2003)]

For Ill Persons Outside Medical Facilities

Artwork created by elders and youngsters for the project, "Soul Shoes," led by *Danceworks*. *Photo by Danceworks, Inc.*

Patients with Parkinson's disease who took part in regular tango dance classes for 20 sessions showed significant improvements in balance and mobility when compared to patients who did conventional exercise. [Hackney, M.E., Kantorovich, S., Levin, R., and Earhart, G.M. "Effects of Tango on Functional Mobility in Parkinson's Disease: A Preliminary Study." *Journal of Neurological Physical Therapy,* 31, 173–179 (2007)]

Using a therapeutic game specifically developed for Alzheimer's disease increased patient pleasure, patient interest, and patient and family member satisfaction. [Cohen, G., Firth, K., Biddle, S., Lewis, M. and Simmens, S. "The First Therapeutic Game Specifically Designed and Evaluated for Alzheimer's Disease." *American Journal of Alzheimer's Disease and Other Dementias,* 23(6), 540-551 (2008)]

Adults with cystic fibrosis who participated in a dance/movement intervention reported significantly greater adherence to nutritional regimens compared to an exercise regimen control group. [Goodill, S. "Research Letter: Dance/Movement Therapy for Adults with Cystic Fibrosis: Pilot Data on Mood and Adherence." *Alternative Therapies in Health and Medicine,* 11(1), 76-77 (2005)]

Individuals with mild to moderate dementia who participated in group reminiscence therapy experienced a greater level of relative well-being as compared to those participating in group activities or unstructured time. [Brooker, D.J., and Duce, L. "Well-Being and Activity in Dementia: A Comparison of Group Reminiscence Therapy, Structured Goal-Directed Activity, And Unstructured Time." *Aging and Mental Health,* 4(4), 354-358 (2000)]

Two Key National Organizations

Founded in 1991, the Society for the Arts in Healthcare advocates for the integration of the arts into the environment and delivery of care within healthcare facilities and provides resources and other assistance to artists and healthcare institutions. It publishes *Arts & Health: An International Journal for Research, Policy and Practice.*

www.thesah.org

The Center for Health Design is a leading nonprofit organization devoted to advancing architecture and healthcare. It publishes *Health Environment Research and Design Journal.*

www.healthdesign.org

After an artist's visit, hospitalized patients were more willing to talk about treatment options with caregivers. [KCI Research and Evaluation. *Satisfaction and Outcomes Assessment, Hospital Artist-In-Residence Program of The Creative Center: Arts for People with Cancer* (2002)]

Including the arts within medical courses has been shown to increase student competencies such as observation, enhancement of counseling skills, and empathy. [Staricoff, R. *Arts and Health: A Review of the Medical Literature.* (London: Arts Council of England, 2004)]

Literature has been proven helpful in developing medical students' empathy across gender, race, class, or culture. [Charon, R., Trauman, B.J., and Conell, J.E. "Literature and Medicine: Contribution to Clinical Practice." *Annals of Internal Medicine,* 122, 599–606 (1995)]

An interviewee talks about his healthcare experiences in the video, *BOOM: Housecalls about Medicine and Graying America.*

Family caregivers of patients with cancer reported a significant reduction in depression, stress, and anxiety, and a significant improvement in overall mood, after participating in an art session. [Walsh, S., Martin, S., and Schmidt, L. "Testing the Efficacy of a Creative-Arts Intervention with Family Caregivers of Patients with Cancer." *Journal of Nursing Scholarship,* 36(3), 214–219 (2004)]

After participating in a two-hour art-making session, family caregivers of patients with cancer experienced decreased salivary cortisol levels. Salivary cortisol levels increase with stress. [Walsh, S.M., Radcliffe, R.S., Castillo, L.C., Kumar, A.M., and Broschard, D.M. "A Pilot Study to Test the Effects of Art-Making Classes for Family Caregivers of Patients with Cancer." *Oncology Nursing Forum,* 34(1), E9–E16 (2007)]

---

1. State of the Field Committee. *State of the Field: Arts in Healthcare 2009.* (Washington, DC: Society for the Arts in Healthcare, 2009)

2. Ibid.

3. Conrad, C., Niess, H., Jauch, K., et al. "Overture for Growth Hormone: Requiem for Interleukin-6?" *Critical Care Medicine,* 35: 2709–2713 (2007)

4. Costandi, Moheb. "Beauty and the Brain." *Seed* (September 16, 2008)

5. Ulrich, Roger. "Effects of Interior Design on Wellness: Theory and Recent Scientific Research." *Journal of Health Care Interior Design,* 3(1): 97-109 (1991)

6. Herndon, Lori. "Take an Artistic Approach to Design." *Healthcare Building Ideas,* 4(4): 40-46 (2008)

7. Wright, Gina. "Hospital Gardens and their Effect on Patients." *Décor & Style* (July, 2001)

8. The Society for the Arts in Healthcare has published a listing of curricula that incorporate the arts. See www.thesah.org

"Throughout this book, we make connections between the worlds of healthcare and the arts by building bridges of understanding based on actual experiences. We have had the privilege of taking you on a journey of 36 stories that describe how a variety of innovative artists have worked with extraordinary healthcare leaders to produce remarkable results. These pioneers have shown us new vistas of what is possible when creativity and compassion work hand in hand, side by side. They provide beacons of hope in an uncertain and often scary world of healthcare."

– page 206

Part II

Exemplary Arts Projects

"Over Me (Good Show)"
Artwork by cancer survivor Susan Wood Reider

"Throughout recorded history, we see evidence that pictures, stories, dances, music, and drama have been central to healing rituals. Today's renewed focus on humanistic care is leading to resurgence in the knowledge and practice of incorporating the arts into healthcare services. Increasing numbers of clinicians and other professionals from the medical community are working side by side with arts professionals in both healthcare and community settings, and around the world the arts are emerging as an important and integral component of healthcare."

– Anita Boles, Executive Director, the Society for the Arts in Healthcare

Imagine...

... that you rush your child, in pain and afraid, to a hospital emergency room.

Art While You Wait program, Hasbro Children's
Hospital, Providence, Rhode Island
Photo by Robin Blossom

You are told it will be a while before your child can be seen. There are others ahead of you.

Your anxiety escalates. Your child is suffering.

A young woman approaches you and invites your child to join other children who are making art projects at a table nearby.

Your child agrees, and a short while later she is engaged in finger-painting, or making and decorating a paper tiara, or coloring with crayons, or any of a very wide range of art projects.

You might feel as these parents did:

"Immediately my child was distracted from her discomfort and fear. I was very grateful that this program was in place this evening."

"I just witnessed my child self-heal before seeing the doctor."

Yes, such a program, called *Art While You Wait*, exists. It serves over 10,000 children each year in eight children's hospitals in the United States, and it has been shown to effectively reduce pain and calm fears in more than 90 percent of children.

It costs a few dollars per child, and some effort, to make it available, yet fewer than ten percent of all children's-hospital emergency waiting rooms offer it or anything like it.

IMAGINE if it were available to all children in all healthcare settings.

This part of the book presents a range of award-winning arts interventions that serve children, adults, and the elderly; that help individuals and families recover from tragedies; and that educate and inform the public about wiser health choices. They address specific needs of cancer patients, expectant mothers, intensive-care patients, family caregivers, the terminally ill, stroke victims, Alzheimer's patients, and many others.

IMAGINE what it might mean to the quality, the humanity, of medical treatment if we just made use of the low-cost, high-impact, arts-based programs currently being used throughout the world to address the pain, suffering, anxiety, and fear caused by illness and injury.

By calming children and parents, *Art While You Wait* also helps the emergency department run more smoothly and efficiently – administrative staff are less besieged by parents wondering when their children will be seen, and the children are better able to respond to the diagnostic questions and activities of medical personnel.

IMAGINE if artists were invited into collaborative relationships with healthcare executives, physicians, patients, and others to create even more programs, and those programs were studied, and the best of them were accepted into our hospitals, clinics, hospices, and communities.

Every day, low-cost, high-impact arts programs are calming, soothing, uplifting, and restoring patients – reducing their suffering, empowering them to move forward, lifting the quality of their days, giving them solace, and supporting those who love them, care for them, and care about them.

But every day is not the same as everywhere. According to recent research, more than half of American hospitals have no arts programs at all.[1] Many of the finest, most effective arts interventions are used in only a handful of places, even though they could be applicable virtually everywhere.

---

1. State of the Field Committee. *State of the Field: Arts in Healthcare 2009.* (Washington, DC: Society for the Arts in Healthcare, 2009)

3

Projects Serving Hospitalized Patients

Part of the "Wing Garden" at the University of Seattle Medical Center, designed by Daniel Winterbottom. *Photo by Daniel Winterbottom*

The case examples in this chapter exemplify the range of ways in which the arts can improve the care that is provided to hospitalized patients. Music, live and recorded, eases pain and suffering and speeds recuperation; art-making reduces pain and other symptoms; and writing enhances many dimensions of wellness. A garden provides solace and rare moments of privacy, and a vivid mural transforms a therapy area from drab to invigorating.

"[T]here is a rich and growing body of research connecting arts in healthcare programs to improved quality of care for patients, their families, and even medical staff. Studies have proven that integrating the arts into healthcare settings helps to cultivate a healing environment, support the physical, mental, and emotional recovery of patients, communicate health and recovery information, and foster a positive environment for caregivers...." *State of the Field: Arts in Healthcare 2009,* Society for the Arts in Healthcare

"Little as we know
about the way in
which we are
affected by form,
by color and light,
we do know this:
They have an actual
physical effect."

– Florence Nightingale

Day hospital collograph

Dreams Art and Health Research Project

Mater Hospital Trust
Belfast, Northern Ireland

In-patient unit monoprint, Psychiatry

A three-year action-research project demonstrates the link between making art and pain reduction.

ac arts care

For three years, from 2003 to 2006, Mater Hospital Trust in Belfast, Northern Ireland hosted an ambitious project aimed at discerning how art-making affects health and well-being. An artist taught a variety of printmaking skills to hospital patients, staff, and other groups, while an external evaluator gathered and assessed data about the effects of the activities. The project was called the *Dreams Art and Health Research Project* (the *Dreams Project*) because the artwork was all developed in relation to the general theme of dreams.

Evaluation was built in from the beginning of the project, which was funded primarily by the Arts Council of Northern Ireland Lottery Project. In the first year an independent evaluator created an overall evaluation strategy; that strategy was deployed in the second year and the results were assessed in the third. A standard questionnaire was used (the Hospital Anxiety and Depression Scale), and another was specially created for the project (the General Enjoyment Survey). Observation, interviews, and video documentation supplemented the paper-and-pencil forms.

The project reported compelling results. Nearly 50 percent of the participants told researchers that their pain and other symptoms were relieved by their art activities. Over 90 percent said they were more relaxed and their moods improved. Ninety percent said they interacted with others in better ways.[1]

Art-Making
Dance
Literary
Media
Music
Performance
Visual

Lorna Hastings

ARTIST PROFILES

The Dreams Project was led by Lorna Hastings, director of Arts Care. It was coordinated by Beverley Healy, who was artist-in-residence at Mater Hospital. In partnership with health trusts throughout Northern Ireland, Arts Care engages 21 artists-in-residence and many project artists, who facilitate and coordinate participatory workshops and performances.

The Dreams Project workshops were led by professional printmaker Anushiya Sundaralingham.

> **"*The Dreams Project* was a culmination of eleven years work for me as the Mater Hospital Artist. The project identified in concrete terms what many of us involved in art and health already knew inside ourselves: that artistic involvement does have a positive impact in a healthcare environment."**
>
> – Beverley Healy

Beverley Healy

Partner Institution

Mater Hospital is one of six facilities within the Belfast Health and Social Care Trust, which has over 22,000 employees. Arts Care, a charitable organization that engages professional artists, is active throughout Northern Ireland and has been involved with Mater Hospital since 1993; *the Dreams Project* was an extension of work already in progress there, with added emphasis on evaluation.

Cancer lifeline group monoprint

"Over the years we have observed the benefits, on many levels, of arts activities on health and we are delighted that the *Dreams* evaluation project has backed up these observations."

– Lorna Hastings

Artworks created by project participants were displayed in annual exhibitions and in printed catalogs.

Cancer lifeline group monoprint

CONTACT INFORMATION

For information about contacting Lorna Hastings at Arts Care, see Appendix A, page 215.

---

1. Gilliland, E., McIldoon, N., and Kelly, J. *Final Report: Evaluation of the Dreams Art and Health Project.* (Belfast, Northern Ireland: Community Evaluation Northern Ireland, 2006)

"The poets did well to conjoin music and medicine, because the office of medicine is but to tune the curious harp of man's body."

– Francis Bacon

A patient is happy that his wife has arrived for a visit so they can waltz together.
Photo by Ruth Powazki and The Cleveland Clinic

Music Therapy in Palliative Medicine

The Harry R. Horvitz Center for Palliative Medicine
at the Cleveland Clinic Taussig Cancer Institute
Cleveland, Ohio

The benefits of music therapy in palliative care are demonstrated by a large and careful study at a leading healthcare institution.

A patient listens intently as a music therapist plays his chosen song of "Misty." *Photo by The Kulas Foundation and Taxel Image Group*

When patients suffer from diseases that are not responsive to curative treatment, their physical pain and psychological distress can be overwhelming. The Cleveland Clinic's response to those circumstances – its Palliative Medicine Program – was recognized by the World Health Organization (WHO) in 1991 as "a unique model of a much-needed service." It now is a WHO Demonstration Project, serving as a model for other care facilities around the world.

Lisa Gallagher has been working in that setting since 1994, providing music therapy to patients and their families and loved ones. In 2000, she began carefully collecting data about the effects of music on the patients she visited. Using several research protocols, she assessed the impacts of one initial music-therapy treatment, lasting about 25 minutes, on a variety of indicators of pain and psychological well-being.[1]

When the information collected from 200 patients (whose ages were between 24 and 87) was analyzed, it showed, at statistically significant levels, that music therapy had beneficial effects on pain, anxiety, depression, shortness of breath, mood, facial expressions, and body movement. 68 family members who participated in the music-therapy sessions also showed significant improvements in mood.

The large number of patients surveyed and the duration of the study, as well as the careful protocols employed, make

Art-Making

Dance

Literary

Media

Music

Performance

Visual

this exemplary research particularly significant. In part as a result of the study, the Cleveland Clinic decided in 2008 to create an Arts & Medicine Institute, expand music therapy throughout the hospital, and further improve the Clinic's overall sound environment.

Dr. Ruth Lagman, Director of Clinical Services for the Horvitz Center for Palliative Medicine, with music therapist Lisa Gallagher as Lisa receives the 2007 Scholarly Activity Award from the Great Lakes Region of the American Music Therapy Association. *Photo by Kathy Hauser*

Music therapist Lisa Gallagher and a patient share a special moment of support during a music therapy session. *Photo by The Kulas Foundation and Taxel Image Group*

"Lisa Gallagher has been carrying the torch for music therapy for many years at Cleveland Clinic in the Palliative Care Unit. The Arts & Medicine Institute is now expanding the music therapy program at Cleveland Clinic on the strong foundation laid by Lisa. Her work combines caring for the patient, conducting research, and educating people on the benefits of music therapy."

– Iva Fattorini, M.D., Executive Director of the Arts & Medicine Institute, Cleveland Clinic

Partner Institution

The Harry R. Horvitz Center for Palliative Medicine at the Cleveland Clinic Taussig Cancer Institute is a 23-bed facility providing inpatient services for acute intensive palliative care for those with cancer and other diseases such as AIDS and ALS. Annual admissions average 700 patients. Hospice and palliative home care are extended to patients at home. The Horvitz Center is a demonstration project for the World Health Organization.

ARTIST PROFILE

Lisa Gallagher
Photo by The Kulas Foundation and Taxel Image Group

Lisa Gallagher is Music Therapy Coordinator for the Cleveland Clinic: she also holds a position with the Clinic's Arts & Medicine Institute.

Trained as a music therapist, she found that she particularly enjoyed working with patients facing difficult circumstances. "I quickly fell in love with using music therapy in healthcare as I saw how it helped patients get through long and sometimes difficult treatments," she says.

"I have always believed that music therapy was powerful, but it was wonderful to see the research and data prove this. I especially found it exciting to show that music therapy is effective in emotional ways – decreasing anxiety and depression and improving mood – but it is also effective in decreasing physical symptoms such as pain and shortness of breath. This was important for the literature and for the profession. I also found it exhilarating and satisfying to know that I had made a difference in the lives of many individuals by helping to distract them from various symptoms, improve their quality of life, and help them in many different ways." – Lisa Gallagher

CONTACT INFORMATION

For information about contacting Lisa Gallagher, see Appendix A, page 215.

"Pain? What pain? I was so excited about the music I forgot about my pain!"

– A patient

---

1. Gallagher, Lisa, et al. "The Clinical Effects of Music Therapy in Palliative Medicine." *Supportive Care in Cancer*, 14: 859-866 (2006)

"It was such a relaxing piece of music that you just went somewhere else. The music was really soothing."

– A heart-procedure patient

Imagery from a MusiCure CD cover

MusiCure and MuViCure

Aarhus University Hospital
Aarhus, Denmark

Specially-designed music calms and soothes patients throughout the world. When used in conjunction with images of nature, the music also has many positive effects.

The first MusiCure CD is a voyage through various landscapes from dawn and into the night.

Beginning in 1998, award-winning composer and musician Niels Eje and a team of musicians and physicians received funding to create new music to improve the overall sound environment in hospitals and for application in specific medical situations.

The team learned all they could about the healing properties of music in order to produce its original recordings. Inge Mulvad Eje, herself a skilled musician, coordinated the project and produced the music on CDs. Five years of pure research and development were undertaken before the first CD was released.

The music they created, now called *MusiCure,* has been rigorously evaluated and shown to have powerful positive effects in a wide range of settings. In studies involving thousands of hospital patients in clinical locations throughout the world, *MusiCure* has been shown to have a relaxing and calming effect on patients during post-operative recovery, on those undergoing invasive cardiography procedures, and in many other environments.[1]

Among four hundred cardiac patients, researchers first asked whether they wanted to listen to music during a procedure they were about to undergo. Sixty percent of those patients said they did not; yet a *MusiCure* CD was played anyway, and ninety-two percent of patients reported that they had liked the sound environment.[2]

Art-Making

Dance

Literary

Media

Music

Performance

Visual

A MusiCure selection can be heard, and MusiCure recordings can be purchased, at www.musicure.com. Information about MuViCure is at www.muvicure.com.

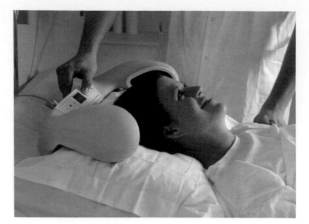

A patient listens to MusiCure.
Photo by Björn Wennerwald

In three psychiatric wards at a hospital in Denmark, patients who normally would have received on-demand medication to alleviate their distress were instead played MusiCure music. The results were dramatic: 87 perpcent of the patients relaxed, calmed down, and even fell asleep from listening to the music, without any medication.[3]

A newer product, MuViCure, incorporates nature imagery with sound images to create islands of calm within therapeutic settings. Testing in a variety of locations, including a nursing-home dementia unit, a rehabilitation facility, and a hospital surgery unit, has shown MuViCure to have positive effects related to anxiety levels, energy, and pain management.[4]

Partner Institution

Aarhus University Hospital, in Aarhus, Denmark, pursues academic and applied research with MusiCure and MuViCure using interdisciplinary methods.

ARTIST PROFILES

Niels Eje was the principal oboe player in the Danish Radio Symphony Orchestra. He has participated in more than 30 CD recordings and toured and performed concerts in the United States, Japan, Denmark, England, Sweden, Mexico, Germany, and France.

Inge Mulvad Eje was trained as a cellist and was a member of the Copenhagen Philharmonic. With Niels Eje, she cofounded Gefion Records and the ensemble Trio Rococo.

"Some of the most rewarding and encouraging experiences we have had during the ten years we have worked with the creation of MusiCure is the immediate positive feedback we receive from patients who spontaneously express how the music has helped them through a difficult time - and it is especially rewarding when after recovery they also express a deep wish to keep using the music on an everyday basis!" - Niels Eje and Inge Eje

Inge Eje and Niels Eje

CONTACT INFORMATION

For information about contacting MusiCure, see Appendix A, page 215.

---

1. See, for example, Thorgaard, P., Ertmann, E., et al. "Designed Sound and Music Environment in Postanaesthesia Care Units—A Multicentre Study of Patients and Staff." *Intensive and Critical Care Nursing*, 21(4): 220-225 (2005); and Nilsson, U., "The Effect of Music Intervention in Stress Response to Cardiac Surgery in a Randomized Clinical Trial." *Heart & Lung: The Journal of Acute and Critical Care*, 37 (2008)

2. Thorgaard, B. "Specially Selected Music in the Cardiac Laboratory—An Important Tool for Improvement of the Well-being of Patients." *European Journal of Cardiovascular Nursing*, 3(1): 21-26B

3. Sørensen, T. and Tyberg, J. "Treatment of Psychiatric Patients Using MusiCure – A Pilot Study." Viewable at www.musicahumana.dk/documents/00022.pdf

4. Research is reported at http://muvicure.com/researchcasestudies.shtml#case2

"All art is autobiographical. The pearl is the oyster's autobiography."

– Federico Fellini

Making Reflective Writing an Integral Part of Healthcare

Shands HealthCare, University of Florida
Health Science Center
Gainesville, Florida

A far-reaching program inspires and utilizes reflective writing by patients, families, staff, and students.

Hello!

Getting your feelings out on paper improves your health. Research shows that writing helps even if you don't show it to anyone. So during your stay at Shands, please use this pad to write about your hopes, fears, dreams, memories, or whatever comes to mind. . .

If you run out of space & need a larger journal, please call Gail K. Ellison AIM Writer-in-Residence Shands ext. 5-0151

SHANDS
Arts in Medicine

Sample journal given to patients when they are admitted to Shands Hospital

Writing down feelings about illness and traumatic events has been shown to benefit health. Reviewing a study involving patients with asthma and rheumatoid arthritis, for example, a medical journalist noted, "The simple act of writing about bad times can be a potent, and low cost, method of relieving pain and symptoms of chronic illnesses."[1]

At Shands HealthCare, which includes eight Florida hospitals, Gail Ellison has indeed put writing into widespread therapeutic use. The cover of a notepad provided to patients reads, "Please use this pad to write about your hopes, fears, dreams, memories, or whatever comes to mind..." On the pages of *Writing for the Health of It* are prompts that encourage the kinds of reflection that promote health. A similar pad is included in a kit that patients may take home from the hospital.

Ellison also has bound writings collected from patients, families, and staff into a booklet, *In-House Wisdom*. She has created specialized writing-related materials for dialysis patients, new mothers, nurses, heart-transplant patients, and others. Her booklet about pets has been very effective: "Everyone who has a pet has a story that other pet owners can relate to – and those stories convey emotions directly related to the human aspects of illness and healing: sadness, happiness, hope, laughter, compassion.... The whole spectrum is there."

Art-Making

Dance

Literary

Media

Music

Performance

Visual

She distributes written materials as widely as possible throughout the Shands system, placing them in waiting areas and dining facilities, posting them on bulletin boards, and providing them in nurses' break rooms. "Anything we can think of to get people to consider writing and to appreciate what others have written, we do," Ellison says.

Since 2003 she has taught an elective course in reflective writing for first- and second-year medical students at the University of Florida College of Medicine. In 2009 she completed a textbook for use in medical-school writing programs.

It's not for nothing that Gail Ellison is called "a Johnny Appleseed of words."

Writing for the Health of It and *Writing in Healthcare Settings* are two examples of the books Gail Ellison has written.

Gail Ellison has created a series of books and materials related to writing in healthcare settings. They are designed for use by patients and staff in hospitals, nursing homes, hospice settings, and other healthcare facilities. They can be viewed and ordered at www.gailellison.com.

Partner Institution

Shands HealthCare, affiliated with the University of Florida Health Science Center, includes eight hospitals: two academic medical centers, four community hospitals, and two specialty hospitals. Shands' Artist-in-Residence program, begun in 1990 as one of the first in the world, is now one of the largest comprehensive arts in healthcare programs anywhere. In 2007 it had 16 paid artists in all art disciplines working in five separate buildings throughout the Shands system.

Gail Ellison

ARTIST PROFILE

Gail Ellison, Ph.D., is Writer in Residence at the Shands Arts in Medicine program.

"The stories I hear from patients and the poems I read aloud with them encompass the entire human experience; they require me to be in there laughing and crying, commiserating and demonstrating optimism – bearing witness and serving as a scribe for posterity.... We are all in this together. We will all know sickness and death and suffer deep loss. We will all experience times of bliss, calmness, and sheer joy. We can all listen, witness, be with, contain, communicate, celebrate, and grieve. Together."

Study shows impact of writing course on medical students

Research conducted by Gail Ellison and Dr. Jolie Haun, funded by the Arnold P. Gold Foundation, assessed the views of medical-school students who took Ellison's writing course between 2003 and 2006. Among the study's findings are the following:

- 78% responded that the course enhanced their ability to practice medicine.

- 80% said that the course helped them learn to listen to viewpoints different from their own.

- 89% said they would recommend the course to other students.[2]

Reflective writing class

CONTACT INFORMATION

For information about contacting Gail Ellison, see Appendix A, page 215.

1. Bovsun, Mara. "Writing Relieves Asthma, Arthritis Pain." *MedServ Medical News* (April 13, 1999), regarding Smyth, J.M., Stone, A.A., Hurewitz, A., and Kaell, A, "Effects of Writing about Stressful Experiences on Symptom Reduction in Patients with Asthma or Rheumatoid Arthritis, A Randomized Trial." *Journal of the American Medical Association*, 281 (1999): 1304-1309

2. Ellison, Gail, and Haun, J. "Reflective Writing in Medical Education: Evaluation of an Elective in the University of Florida College of Medicine." www.gailellison.com

"Music is a higher revelation than all wisdom and philosophy. Music is the electrical soil in which the spirit lives, thinks and invents."

– Beethoven

Bedside Harp instructional class taking place
in the lobby of RWJUH Hamilton, 2004
Photo property of Bedside Harp

Bedside Harp

Robert Wood Johnson University Hospital
Hamilton, New Jersey

Live harp music benefits patients in a wide variety of healthcare settings.

Edie Elkan with a patient
Photo property of Bedside Harp

In 2001, Edie Elkan's husband went into the hospital for what was supposed to be a routine surgical procedure – but he wound up in intensive care, on life support. She sat at his bedside every day playing harp music to him as he progressed from the ICU to a step-down unit and then into rehabilitation.

She explains what her playing accomplished:

> My music, I found, did far more that just relax him; indeed, the monitors he was attached to offered irrefutable evidence that within minutes of my playing, his oxygen absorption levels increased, his heart rate was lowered, and his blood pressure fell into normal ranges! When he returned home I asked him what he thought the music did for him during his hospitalization. "It calmed and soothed me," he answered, "and on my darkest days, it gave me hope to go on."

"That did it for me," she says. "I knew then that my dream program had to be run out of a hospital – but how on earth would I get through the door?"

She had been trying for some time to gain regular opportunities to play her harp in healthcare facilities, and she had approached a hospice, a rehabilitation center, and a nursing home, but they all had turned down the idea of an ongoing music program.

She persisted, and later in 2001 she met Sheila Bimbaum, who was the patient relations coordinator of the Robert Wood Johnson University Hospital in Hamilton, New Jersey. Bimbaum asked Elkan to come play there for a few hours.

Art-Making

Dance

Literary

Media

Music

Performance

Visual

After playing, Elkan told Bimbaum about her dream to have a base within a hospital, and Bimbaum answered without hesitation, "Oh yes, you absolutely must do it here."

Patient satisfaction scores zoomed up, and other hospitals took notice. Now, through the program she named *Bedside Harp*, Elkan and her students have provided thousands of hours of harp therapy at the five hospitals in New Jersey and Pennsylvania that host the program. They have taught more than five hundred people to play the harp for their own healing, and trained over fifty people to play the harp in medical environments.

Extensive research has demonstrated the efficacy of live harp music to reduce anxiety among patients undergoing chemotherapy, to soothe premature infants, as a palliative intervention for hospice patients, and in many other settings.[1]

Bedside Harp harpists playing in the lobby of RWJUH Hamilton, 2003.
Photo property of Bedside Harp

Edie Elkan with a patient
Photo property of Bedside Harp

"An older man was seated in a geri chair looking a little uncomfortable. Standing around him were three adult daughters, one of whom said, 'Look, Dad, a harp!' and asked me in. She said he had no preferences so I played some familiar songs. Everyone was smiling and one daughter leaned over the back of the chair with her arm around his neck; one was swaying to the music. As I started to back out of the room the patient said, 'Can you play 'Danny Boy'?' I started into it slowly and in seconds, two of the girls were in tears. He was smiling and moving his foot to the music. He thanked me and said, 'Bless you' as I left. A bit later, one daughter came to me at the elevator and said, 'You made a truly beautiful moment back there for my family.'" – Edie Elkan

Partner Institution

Robert Wood Johnson University Hospital Hamilton, in Hamilton, New Jersey, provides comprehensive acute care and outpatient services. RWJUH Hamilton, the only New Jersey hospital to receive the prestigious Malcolm Baldridge National Quality Award, is part of the Robert Wood Johnson Health Network, an alliance of leading local healthcare providers throughout central New Jersey. The network includes 13 hospitals and health centers and numerous satellite facilities.

ARTIST PROFILE

Edie Elkan
Photo property of Bedside Harp

Edie Elkan is founding director of *Bedside Harp*, a college-based, hospital-hosted harp therapy program based in Bensalem, Pennsylvania. Elkan, a classically trained harpist, returned to playing the instrument for her own healing after three people in her life died within eight months of each other. "I am taking music to the highest place I can think of," states Elkan. "When you see a patient with Alzheimer's disease – who hasn't spoken for months – sit up and begin to sing, how can you walk away and not think that was the most important moment of your life?"

Excerpt from the *Bedside Harp* Oath of Service, composed by Edie Elkan:

I swear to fulfill, to the best of my ability and judgment, this covenant:

I will use my harp to the best of my ability to serve those who call me to their side.

I will treat all whom I serve with honor, warmth, understanding, compassion and love.
I and each person I serve are equals – we are, each of us, connected to the other.
All suffering is like my suffering; all joy is like my joy.

I commit myself to a lifetime of learning and professional and personal growth.
My training and experience will be used to benefit all whom I serve.

I will remember that service is the work of the soul, resting on the premise that life is a holy mystery whose purpose is unknown.

I will respect the hard-won gains of those who have brought music and other arts to healthcare, those who have gone before me and in whose steps I walk. I will gladly share such knowledge as is mine with those who are to follow.

"You turned my day around. I was feeling so sorry for myself I didn't know what to do. You made me hope I could get better. Thank you."

– A patient

CONTACT INFORMATION

For information about contacting Edie Elkan at Bedside Harp, see Appendix A, page 215.

---

1. Many studies are cited at www.bedsideharp.com/BSH/research.htm.

"Art condenses the experience we all have as human beings, and, by forming it, makes it significant. We all have an in-built need for harmony and the structures that create harmony. Basically, art is an affirmation of life."

– Trevor Bell

View into the garden with the red planter
Photo by Daniel Winterbottom

The Wing Garden

University of Washington Medical Center
Seattle, Washington

A rooftop garden offers solace, privacy, and options to hospital patients.

Hospital staff use the garden on a regular basis.
Photo by Daniel Winterbottom

A woman confined to bed in a maternity ward for high-risk patients at the University of Washington Medical Center, allowed out of bed only once each day, used that time to meet her husband at dusk in the Medical Center's rooftop *Wing Garden* so they could, in her words, "watch the sunset in our secret refuge."

The garden, designed by Daniel Winterbottom and his students at the University of Washington's department of landscape architecture, provides solace, inspiration, and relaxation for patients. Its unique design, with four separate areas, allows for privacy and multiple overall uses of the same general space. Winterbottom describes an additional benefit from the multiple areas: "For patients, being able to choose among a variety of spaces is a precious freedom in a place where choices are so constrained."

That feeling of freedom while in the garden is one of many features that Winterbottom incorporated into the design after extensive interaction with patients, visitors, staff, and administrators during the design phase. Saturated colors contrast with much of the hospital's interior décor, curvilinear forms are a counterpoint to the rectangularity inside the facility, plants offer a variety of scents and attract wildlife, and views of Puget Sound and surrounding hills promote relaxed contemplation. "For me," Winterbottom says, "the garden represents a transformation from a place where care is administered to a caring place."

Art-Making

Dance

Literary

Media

Music

Performance

Visual

Research shows that well-designed garden areas within hospitals and other healthcare facilities have significant impacts on the well-being of many populations. As one seminal study reported, "95 percent of the people in gardens reported a therapeutic benefit. Employees said they were more productive, patients spoke of feeling better and having more tolerance for their medical procedures, and friends and relatives felt relief from the stress of the hospital visit."[1]

Visiting mother and son: The son is a patient and they use the garden every day.
Photo by Daniel Winterbottom

Curved seating allows people in wheelchairs to pull up and converse with friends, visitors, and staff.
Photo by Daniel Winterbottom

Daniel Winterbottom is developing a therapeutic park for children in a squatters' community working in a garbage dump in Guatemala City. His future international projects include therapeutic gardens for disabled children in Bosnia and a medical clinic and therapeutic gardens for an orphanage in Uganda.

Partner Institution

Rated by *U.S. News & World Report* as one of America's top hospitals in every year since the magazine began evaluating hospitals in 1990, the University of Washington Medical Center has also earned "Magnet Hospital" designation by the American Nurses Credentialing Center for eighteen consecutive years, and was named an environmental leader by Hospitals for a Healthy Environment.

ARTIST PROFILE

Daniel Winterbottom is associate professor in the department of landscape architecture at the University of Washington, and adjunct associate professor in the department of architecture there. A registered landscape architect, he is the principal of Winterbottom Design, a Seattle-based landscape architecture and site-planning firm. His academic and professional work focuses on therapeutic environments, and includes a hospice garden, a garden for disabled adults, and a playgarden for disabled children.

"In 1991, when my mother was diagnosed with ovarian cancer, I saw how the cold, invasive, and depersonalized hospital surroundings impeded our attempts to reach closure. The gathering places lacked privacy, intimacy, and character, augmenting our frustration and sadness. Only during drives in the country and visits in our home garden were we able to relax and confide in each other. These experiences propelled my efforts to create meaningful, supportive, and nurturing environments in the healthcare setting." – Daniel Winterbottom

Daniel Winterbottom

"At the local, national, and international levels there is a growing need for therapeutic environments and awareness about the benefits is increasing. Evidence shows that nature interactions can help people to overcome traumas caused by war, poverty, abuse, and incarceration. As we seek to become a more compassionate and supportive society, environments that nurture are critical in healthcare, schools, institutions, and communities in need." – *Daniel Winterbottom*

View into the garden with the blue metal "green" wall that provides privacy *Photo by Daniel Winterbottom*

CONTACT INFORMATION

For information about contacting Daniel Winterbottom, see Appendix A, page 215.

1. Marcus, Clare, and Barnes, M. *Healing Gardens: Therapeutic Benefits and Design Recommendations* (New York: John Wiley, 1999).

"Art is our memory of love.
The most an artist can do through
their work is say, let me show you
what I have seen, what I have loved,
and perhaps you will see it and love it too."

– Annie Bevan

The "Kites" Mural

Chelsea and Westminster Hospital NHS Foundation Trust
London, England

A bright mural enlivens a drab hospital area and helps designers learn about the effects of both color and design.

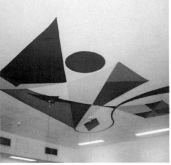

The ceiling above the hydrotherapy pool is a key focal point in the design.

When Jane Duncan received a commission to create a mural for the hydrotherapy room at Chelsea and Westminster Hospital, she did not take her assignment lightly. "It is a colorist's dream to be asked to design a mural for this stark white space, which lacked any sense of identity or energy," she says.

She also liked another aspect of the assignment – that it was conducted as part of a long-term research project on the impact of color and design on patients, a subject she had pondered for some time. Since the goal of the mural was to inspire physical activity and create a supportive environment for patients and staff, she selected a palette of nine hues that had been shown by emerging research to be associated with action, movement, and happiness. "I wanted to use color to achieve a dynamic environment for the patients in the hydrotherapy room, to encourage them to move and exercise. I also wanted them to feel cheerful," she says.[1]

The design linked bold colors and geometric shapes to form a continuous abstract pattern across the walls, with a complementary design of kites on the ceiling. The designs and colors were carefully positioned to aid the staff during treatment, and special attention was given to the ceiling because it was a focal point for many patients, particularly children with special needs, many of whom are treated while supine in the water.

Art-Making

Dance

Literary

Media

Music

Performance

Visual

A three-stage evaluation was employed to assess patients' reactions: before the change, one month later, and three months later. After three months, 68 percent of patients evaluated the change to the hydrotherapy room as being for the better.

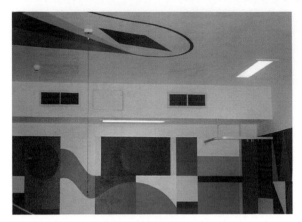

Kite murals on the surrounding wall and ceiling

Staff reported that they found the colors and designs helpful as a focal point when treating anxious patients, particularly children. Duncan also investigated patients' reactions to specific colors that had been shown by previous research using Nobbs Color Emotional Scales to be associated with action and movement; the colors used in the murals proved to be consistent with the Nobbs Scales.

"Why, when people are sick, often at their lowest ebb in life, should they also be subjected to a non-supportive environment? Why should the quality of the environment not match the standards of medical care?"

– Jane Duncan

The colors and geometric designs on the surrounding walls provide an additional focal point for patients, and help create a vibrant and stimulating environment for both patients and staff.

Partner Institution

Opened in 1993, Chelsea and Westminster Hospital is part of the Imperial College School of Medicine and a teaching center for Thames Valley University in Nursing. The hospital has a very large and active arts program, including visual and performing arts.

Jane Duncan
Photo by Chris Harding

ARTIST PROFILE

Jane Duncan, who holds a degree in public art and design, co-authored the pioneering 2002 report, "A Study of the Effects of the Visual and Performing Arts in Healthcare."[2] She has been an artist in residence at the Centre for Medical Humanities, University College London, where she was also a part-time lecturer.

She is currently managing director of Public Art & Design Consultancy, and an editorial advisor and journalist for the UK publication, *Art & Architecture Journal*. In 2007, her further pioneering research, "A Cluster Designed Controlled Trial of Arts-Based Observational Skills Training In Primary Care," was published in the *Medical Education Journal*.

"Like most cultural influences of any lasting significance, the field of arts and health has undergone significant changes in recent years. Being a pioneer in the field has meant being willing to take a risk, in order to help transform the future. To quote Ralph Waldo Emerson – 'Do not go where the path may lead, go instead where there is no path and leave a trail.'" –Jane Duncan

CONTACT INFORMATION

For information about contacting Jane Duncan, see Appendix A, page 215.

---

1. For more information, see Duncan, Jane, "The Effect of Colour and Design in Hydrotherapy: Designing for Care," in Kirklin, Deborah and Ruth Richardson, eds. *The Healing Environment: Without and Within* (London: Royal College of Physicians of London, 2003): 81-100

2. Staricoff, Rosalia, Jane Duncan, and Melissa Wright. "A Study of the Effects of the Visual and Performing Arts in Healthcare." Viewable at http://chelwestcharity.org.uk/binary_data/263_study_visual_performing_arts.pdf

"Where words fail,
music speaks."

– Hans Christian Andersen

Virtual Music Maker

Beth Israel Deaconess Medical Center
Boston, Massachusetts

Creating music through their own rehabilitative movements helps stroke victims recover faster and better.

Dr. Amir Lahav operates the Virtual Music Maker, an interactive human-computer interface that converts body movements into real-time auditory feedback.

For stroke victims, physical rehabilitation is often arduous, frustrating, dispiriting work. Movements, small and large, that once came easily can often only be restored through specific, highly-disciplined exercises performed with dutiful regularity.

Dr. Amir Lahav, a professional musician and rehabilitation scientist, wondered whether music might help patients persevere with their treatments and repeat the precise rehabilitative movements with more accuracy, leading to faster improvement.

At the core of his idea was not just any music, but music actually created by the rehabilitating patients themselves while performing their exercises. Along with an interdisciplinary team at Boston University and Harvard Medical School's Beth Israel Deaconess Medical Center, Lahav developed the *Virtual Music Maker*, a computer-based auditory feedback device that translates movements into sounds.

In therapy focused on recovering hand motor function, a stroke patient might be required, for example, to execute certain therapeutic hand movements in order to keep a prerecorded musical selection playing, or to create a new melody, or to change the volume of the music.[1]

In a pilot test on a small group of stroke victims, Lahav and his colleagues demonstrated that patients exercising with the aid of Virtual Music Maker achieved hand movements that were more controlled, coordinated, and purposeful than those of patients receiving traditional nonmusical therapy.[2] Additional assessment of the participants in the pilot study showed that in addition to improved motor function, they experienced increased self-esteem and a higher quality of life. Lahav reports, "Overall, the music making group were all highly motivated to continue with therapy and even considered the possibility of taking music lessons."

Art and science combine in *Virtual Music Maker* for the betterment of patients – and a vivid glimpse into some of what the future can hold in the hands of committed teams of artists and scientists.

Patients learn to play music by performing prescribed occupational therapy exercises targeting functional everyday movements.

A subject performs the "Play a Rhythm" exercise with a four-region rhythm instruments display. At the instance shown, most of the hand pixels appear in the lower-left region of the display, covering the drum, which is therefore selected.

Playing the Music Maker does not require special musical talent, and is possible even for patients with very limited movement.

"Music is well said to be the speech of angels."

– Thomas Carlyle

Partner Institution

Beth Israel Deaconess Medical Center (BIDMC) in Boston is a teaching and research hospital affiliated with Harvard Medical School. Hosting nearly 750,000 patient visits annually, BIDMC is known for excellence in many disciplines.

ARTIST PROFILE

Amir Lahav, Ph.D., is a professional musician and composer who combines his musical skills with neuroscience and clinical research. He holds a bachelor's degree in music, a master's degree in exercise science, and a doctoral degree in rehabilitation science.

In 2008, he began working as an assistant professor in the Department of Newborn Medicine at the Brigham and Women's Hospital at Harvard Medical School. Of that assignment, he says, "I will be directing a new clinical initiative aimed at developing an audio-friendly incubator to examine the effects of music, mixed with sounds from the womb and recordings of the baby's mother's voice, on the growth and neurodevelopment of premature infants."

He also plans to continue his research on auditory feedback therapies for stroke patients through a secondary affiliation with Spaulding Rehabilitation Hospital, a teaching hospital of Harvard Medical School.

"Imagine a future in which individuals are personally responsible for the betterment of their health, merely by interacting with creative tools.... In the future, we all hope to see more interactive musical devices used in clinical settings, and more brain imaging studies showing that such therapy is indeed effective."

Amir Lahav

CONTACT INFORMATION

For information about contacting Amir Lahav, see Appendix A, page 215.

---

1. For further information, see Gorman, M., Betke, M., Saltzman, E., and Lahav, A. "Music Maker – A Camera-Based Rehabilitation Tool for Physical Rehabilitation." *Boston University Computer Science Technical Report No. 2005-032* (www.cs.bu.edu/techreports/pdf/2005-032-music-maker.pdf)

2. $40,000 for conducting the study of stroke victims was provided by the Grammy Foundation of the National Academy of Recording Arts and Sciences, which gives out the annual Grammy Awards.

Projects Serving Children

Hallie and her mom read *Oodles of Doodles*. *Photo by Richard Brown*

All children enter a potentially terrifying world of pain and disease they cannot really understand, treatments that can be painful and frightening, decisions made for and about them by people they don't know. Psychological studies have shown that as many as 30 percent of hospitalized children can suffer severe psychological disturbances and upward of 90 percent of them experience some emotional upset. Their parents or caregivers often are frightened and suffering, too – and their siblings are not immune from emotional conflicts.

The case examples in this chapter show how the arts can help reduce pain and stress, add joy and wonder, and help family members, building crucially-important bridges between the medical experience and the human experience.

"Children need a safe way to communicate their anxieties, and often the best way to cope can be found in the trappings of childhood: crayons, paper, paint, clay. Children and adolescents don't always have words to express what they are going through and are typically creative by nature.... Activities based in creative art therapies engage them in a process that builds self-esteem as well as problem solving and life skills. Their creativity helps them access and explore pent-up emotions." – *Art with Heart*

"*Oodles of Doodles* is a wonderful piece of art and literature that stimulates the users' creativity and builds their self-esteem. Perhaps more importantly, the activities in the book – thoughtfully designed and masterfully illustrated – allow users to see beyond their stay in the hospital to life after their treatment. As an organization focused on living with, through, and beyond cancer, the Lance Armstrong Foundation can appreciate the benefit this book will have for the quality of life of chronically ill children."

– Lance Armstrong Foundation

"Dirty Fingers"
Photo by Richard Brown

Oodles of Doodles

Art with Heart
Seattle, Washington

Hallie hugging her *Oodles* book
Photo by Richard Brown

Famous artists illustrate a therapeutic book of activities for hospitalized children.

healing kids through creativity

In 1996, graphic designer Steffanie Lorig was elected to the board of directors of the Seattle Chapter of the American Institute of Graphic Arts and chosen to chair the board's community outreach committee. She named the committee "Art with Heart," and proceeded to expand its outreach to needy children in the Seattle area.

At first, most of the committee's activities focused on homeless children. The Intergenerational Book Project, for example, brought homeless children together with senior citizens to write and illustrate storybooks.

Then in 1999, Lorig met a young girl with cancer, Hallie Holton, and that night Lorig had a dream about a book that would bring happiness and contentment to hospitalized children.

After two and a half years of planning and development, Lorig's dream resulted in *Oodles of Doodles*, which provides therapeutic activities for hospitalized chronically- and seriously-ill children. Lorig arranged for over 40 artists from around the world to create vivid illustrations for the therapeutic activities in the book, which has been recognized for its excellence by the Make-A-Wish Foundation, the Starlight Foundation for Children, the Society for the Arts in Healthcare, and the Lance Armstrong Foundation, among others.

The activities in the book are designed, in Lorig's words, "to encourage these special children to express themselves through imagination and creativity, providing a non-threatening outlet for fear and anxiety." They include empowerment activities, creating a cartoon, designing a personal

Art-Making
Dance
Literary
Media
Music
Performance
Visual

robot, imagination stations, and making tags for their IV poles. The children can express their wishes, hopes, and fears and let visitors and medical personnel know how they are feeling.

Art with Heart gave away the first 20,000 copies of *Oodles of Doodles* to hospitals; now the book is offered at a nominal charge, with discounts for bulk orders. Within five years after its publication, *Oodles of Doodles* had reached over 36,000 children in more than 500 hospitals across North America. It also has been published in Spanish.

Lorig's *Oodles* books
Photo by Jim Linna

Sarah Wilson's drawing
Photo by Richard Brown

Draw a picture showing how this book made you feel.

Sarah Wilson
Age: 11 ½
I am in the hospital because I have leukimia

"Being sick is really hard for kids, and being in the hospital is even worse. Whatever we can do to make it better is worth doing. This is just a small contribution toward making a child smile and feel a little bit better, when smiling isn't always an easy thing to do."

– **Mary Grand Pré, illustrator of the *Harry Potter* books and contributor to *Oodles of Doodles***

Dear Oodles Doodles,
                This book made me feel happy. it is so Fun. Their Posters, and book marks, and everything. It is cool.
   I had 18 Surgeays, when I got this book, I was in the bed, and I did this book, It Took the Pain away, while I was doing it. It is So cool.
   I wisn I had a nother book, I am already done with it.

I know I can't drow good. But!!
I don't care.

Victoria's letter
Photo by Richard Brown

ARTIST PROFILE

Steffanie Lorig
Photo by Jim Linna

Before she began Art with Heart, Steffanie Lorig was an award-winning graphic designer, art director, and author.

"My involvement in the *Oodles* project changed many aspects of my life – including my career – but on a much more important and critical level, it is changing the lives of children all around the world, and I am humbled by that amazing fact on a daily basis."

"This project was blessed from the beginning. Miracles occurred almost daily, as funding appeared from nowhere, paper mills called out of the blue to offer free paper, six printers agreed to split the job for cost, and artists who had never heard of us trusted us with their gifts." –Steffanie Lorig

Oodles core team, bottom left to right: Terry Marks and Steffanie Lorig, top row left to right: Dororthee, Andrew, and Peggie
Photo by Chuck Brown

CONTACT INFORMATION

For information about contacting Steffanie Lorig at Art with Heart,
see Appendix A, page 215.

Beyond *Oodles of Doodles*

Art with Heart has followed *Oodles of Doodles* with other important publications and projects.

Chill and Spill is a therapeutic journal for adolescents dealing with crisis, supported by a manual and training program for child life therapists, social workers, and other professionals, to teach them the best uses of the book. In a substantial study of therapists using *Chill and Spill* with teenagers who were described as "hard to communicate with" and "anxious" (two-thirds of whom had been expelled from school and were considered to have significant behavior problems), 38 percent of the therapists said that the book helped reduce symptoms of depression and that the teens were easier to communicate with after using the book; 50 percent reported that it increased the teens' personal insights; and 75 percent said it allowed for greater expression of self.

The book *Magnificent Marvelous Me!* grew out of Art with Heart's Sibling Project, which helps meet the emotional needs of siblings of the seriously ill and disabled. Those siblings often feel neglected, angry, and undervalued. Like *Oodles of Doodles, Magnificent Marvelous Me!* is illustrated by many volunteer professional artists from around the world.

"Art must do something more than give pleasure. It should relate to our own life so as to increase our energy of spirits."

– Kenneth Clark

A nature-themed diorama project acts as a therapeutic distraction while patients wait for medical treatment.
Photo by Robin Blossom

Art While You Wait

Hasbro Children's Hospital
Providence, Rhode Island

Art projects ease fears and reduce pain amid the stresses of children's hospital emergency departments.

A young patient proudly displays his finished paper bag puppet.
Photo by Kyle McDonald

A child in the waiting area of a hospital emergency department can be required to endure hours of pain and fear. Parents' nerves can jangle, too. At Hasbro Children's Hospital in Providence, Rhode Island, and in several other hospitals across the United States, *Art While You Wait* changes that.

In this program a facilitator approaches children and the adults accompanying them, and invites the children to participate in an arts activity. For those who participate, research indicates that over 90 percent are helped to forget their pain, concern, or anxiety. 100 percent of the children in one survey answered yes to the question, "Do you think doing an art project is a good thing to do while waiting for the doctor?" The children become so committed to their art works that they often bring them into treatment rooms with them.

Parents' relief is observable, too. One wrote of the program, "It was a life saver! Thank you for your sweet attention to my little lady."

By calming children and parents, *Art While You Wait* also helps the emergency department run more smoothly and efficiently. Administrative staff are less besieged by parents wondering when their children will be seen, and the children are better able to respond to the diagnostic questions and activities of medical personnel.

In 2009, *Art While You Wait*, which is a program of the Art for Life Foundation, had been implemented in seven hospitals in seven states.

Art-Making

Dance

Literary

Media

Music

Performance

Visual

Kyle McDonald
Photo by Karim Hamid

ARTIST PROFILE

Kyle McDonald started the first Artist-in-Residence program at Children's Hospital in Oakland, California, which became part of the family of programs at the Art for Life Foundation. She now directs the *Art While You Wait* program in Hasbro's emergency department, and also a similar program in the hospital's neurological development clinic.

She is also a painter. Samples of her work can be seen at www.dolbychadwickgallery.com.

"One can really see the difference in the kids. I see a physical difference and an emotional one, and I know the creative process definitely contributes to a movement toward healing in your mind, body, and soul."

Art While You Wait **was created by Anthony Knutson, the founder of the *Art for Life Foundation*. In 2009, *Art for Life's* programs reached close to 20,000 children.**

A typical evening of art-making in the emergency waiting area at the Hasbro Children's Hospital in Providence, Rhode Island.
Photo by Robin Blossom

"Very impressive. I just witnessed my child self-heal before seeing the doctor."

– Parent

Partner Institution

Hasbro Children's Hospital is the pediatric division of Rhode Island Hospital. The Emergency Department sees up to 50,000 patients each year.

"As a child I was hospitalized frequently due to severe asthma. Occasionally I was well enough to go to the activity room. My fondest memory is of an old wooden easel stocked with bright cups of paint, waiting for my brush! That little slice of heaven left an indelible impression in my mind. As an adult, I often felt the desire to volunteer in a children's hospital and offer art and craft activities to patients. I left my career as a fashion designer, went to graduate school, and earned my MFA in painting with a focus on arts and consciousness." – Kyle McDonald

Student intern Alysha Polite navigates the *Art While You Wait* cart to the emergency department waiting area.
Photo by Kyle McDonald

"In *Art While You Wait*, children become a part of a nurturing environment where they can express themselves. Art provides a passage of joy that allows children the chance to transform their lives on their journey from illness into wellness."

– Anthony Knutson

"Immediately my child was distracted from her discomfort and fear, and actively engaged in an arts project. I was very grateful that this program was in place this evening."

– Parent

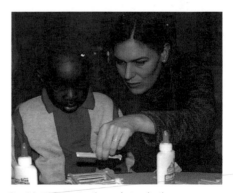

Popsicle stick construction project under the guidance of Kyle McDonald
Photo by Robin Blossom

CONTACT INFORMATION

For information about contacting Art for Life Foundation or Kyle McDonald, see Appendix A, page 215.

"Rhythm and harmony find their way into the inward places of the soul."

– Plato

Musical instruments, books, and toys
used in musical therapy
Photo by Judy Nguyen Engel

Pediatric Procedural Support Program

Tallahassee Memorial HealthCare
Tallahassee, Florida

Musical instruments used in musical therapy
Photo by Judy Nguyen Engel

Live music virtually eliminates the need for pharmaceutical sedation of children facing noninvasive medical procedures.

A mother writes:

> I brought my three-year-old son to the hospital for an echocardiogram. Because of extensive hospital stays during his first year of life, he was anxious when we arrived. Within fifteen minutes, Miriam arrived with her guitar. My son visibly relaxed and followed her happily to the exam room. The hour-long test was pure enjoyment for my son and myself.

"I cannot express my relief and my gratitude for our wonderful visit," she concluded. "Thank you from a grateful mother's heart."

The hospital was Tallahassee Memorial. Miriam is one of the music therapists the hospital employs to sing or play soothing music with children who become anxious when facing a forthcoming noninvasive medical procedure, such as an echocardiogram or CT scan.

Previously, children who became too anxious before undergoing medical tests had been pharmaceutically sedated by an anesthesiologist so the test could proceed. In the *Pediatric Procedural Support Program* at Tallahassee Memorial, live music played or sung to the anxious children by a skilled music therapist has been sufficiently calming to allow the test to proceed without anesthesia. The hospital has eliminated anesthesia 98 percent of the time for echocardiograms and 88 percent for CT scans, with no need at all for sedation of children under the age of six.

The musical interventions in this context average fifteen to thirty minutes, while pharmaceutical sedation of young patients requires an average of about two hours. The musictherapy strategy also requires far fewer resources: anesthesia requires an anesthesiologist, a separate room for sedation and recovery, and a nurse who is present during the entire sedation period. The risks associated with anesthetizing a patient are eliminated, and staff can be deployed in more effective ways. A 2008 journal article showed the practical consequences of the program and the implications for its wider adoption:

> Tallahassee Memorial HealthCare, using the arts during the preparation period for pediatric CT scans, saved $567 per procedure, put three hours of nursing time back on the floors, reduced the medications needed by the young patients, cut down on overnight stays…. With at least four million CT scans performed annually on children alone, the potential cost savings for this single procedure exceeds $2.25 billion.[1]

The use of music to calm anxious patients has also been extended to the insertion of intravenous lines in children, reducing anxiety during MRI scans in adults and children, and other applications.

Musical instruments used in musical therapy
Photo by Judy Nguyen Engel

"Parents are always amazed at how well music therapy works. Many times they are very skeptical that it will work for their child, but in the end the child and the parent leave happy."

– Lisa Mullee, former Cardiovascular Lab Director, Tallahassee Memorial Hospital

"I have witnessed the effects of music therapy on patients, family, and staff. I have seen the positive effects of music therapy on my staff during weekly staff 'motivational moments.' It increases staff morale, rapport, motivation, knowledge of music therapy services for patients, and enhances the overall work environment. Music therapy has also received praise from general inpatients and family members."

– Mark O'Bryant, President & CEO, Tallahassee Memorial HealthCare

Musical instruments
Photo by Judy Nguyen Engel

Partner Institution

Tallahassee Memorial Hospital, a 770-bed acute care facility and the eighth largest hospital in Florida, is part of Tallahassee Memorial HealthCare. Its medical music therapy department was founded in 1999, in partnership with the Florida State University College of Music.

Judy Nguyen Engel

ARTIST PROFILE

Judy Nguyen Engel coordinated the Pediatric Procedural Support Program at Tallahassee Memorial Hospital from 2002 to 2007. She is vice president-elect of the American Music Therapy Association – New England Region. Through her company, Engel Music Therapy, in New Canaan, Connecticut, she provides music therapy services to premature and full-term infants from birth to two years old. She is a Fellow at the National Institute for Infant and Child Medical Music Therapy at Florida State University, which provides training and guidance for institutions and individuals interested in pediatric procedural support and related programs.

"I believe the use of music therapy is an effective approach to meeting the needs of patients and families. This approach should not be considered as an alternative therapeutic tool, but as a standard for all care. Using music therapy as an intervention can create a positive rapport with patients and families; present opportunities to communicate emotions and process feelings; provide potential for self-expression, autonomy, support, and distraction; facilitate exploration of alternative coping skills; and offer a medium for healing and comfort."

The Pediatric Procedural Support Program was created by Darcy DeLoach Walworth, Ph.D. She currently is on the faculty of Florida State University, where she researches the effects of music therapy in medical and early childhood settings with emphases in medical procedural support, autism treatment, and developmental outcomes of premature infants. She has published many articles in music therapy and nursing journals and has contributed chapters to and co-authored music therapy books.

Darcy DeLoach Walworth, Ph.D.

CONTACT INFORMATION

For information about contacting Judy Nguyen Engel or the Pediatric Procedural Support program at Tallahassee Memorial Hospital, see Appendix A, page 215.

---

1. Wood, Beverly P. "CT Scans and Radiation Exposure." *AAP Grand Rounds* 19: 28-29 (2008)

"Music is the language of the spirit. It opens the secret of life bringing peace, abolishing strife."

– Khalil Gibran

Laura Corlin proudly displays her Sadler Award.
Photo by Pat Corlin

The Difference Music Makes

St. Jude Children's Research Hospital
Memphis, Tennessee

Laura Corlin performs at Dartmouth
Hitchcock Children's Hospital.
Photo by Pat Corlin

A young woman's determined efforts bring music to thousands of hospitalized children.

In 2002, when she was fifteen years old, Laura Corlin was challenged by an adult friend to do something for hospitalized children.

Helping others was not new for her. When she was six, she and her sister organized a campaign, "Help Someone Live Better with a Sweater," that has since collected over 10,000 sweaters for needy families in New Hampshire, where she lives. She also organized a regular local talent showcase that has raised $30,000 for the Muscular Dystrophy Association.

Selecting St. Jude Children's Research Hospital in Memphis as the first locale for her challenge to help hospitalized children, she pondered what to do. She recalled her recent experience of the final days of her grandfather, Charles Kennedy:

> I loved to sing to him, especially toward the end when I wasn't sure if he could hear me anymore. He hadn't really responded to any of us in a while, and suddenly when I was singing to him one day he blinked and squeezed my hand. I just knew he was trying to tell me he heard me. My music seemed to make the difference.

An accomplished singer who had been appearing in stage productions since she was very young, Corlin decided to record children's songs that she sang herself for the young patients at St. Jude's. With production help from her singing teacher, she recorded a CD, "The Difference Music Makes."

That was only the beginning. She arranged to perform live at St. Jude's in August of 2003, and by the time she arrived she had sold enough copies of her CD that she could donate 500 of them to the hospital and donate the proceeds from the

Art-Making

Dance

Literary

Media

Music

Performance

Visual

Corlin performs at Rady Children's Hospital.
Photo by Pat Corlin

sale of 500 more. She brought over 700 more CDs, donated by other musicians and music stores, and she brought 30 donated CD players.

That, too, was only a beginning. Through Corlin's persistent efforts, over $35,000 worth of CDs, CD players, and cash contributions have been provided to children's hospitals throughout the United States. Two additional CDs featuring her and other artists have been created: "Tru Colors" and "Tru Holidays." The project has earned honors that include the Kids Who Care Award, Youth Venture Award, and United Way Spirit of Community Award.

"Take a music bath once or twice a week for a few seasons. You will find it is to the soul what a water bath is to the body."

– Oliver Wendell Holmes

Laura Corlin shares "The Difference Music Makes" with second-graders.
Photo by Pat Corlin

Partner Institution

St. Jude Children's Research Hospital opened in 1962 and is now recognized as one of the world's premier centers for study and treatment of catastrophic diseases in children. St. Jude has treated children from all fifty states and from around the world, accepted by physician referral because the children had newly diagnosed diseases that were under research at St. Jude. Ability to pay has not been an issue for admittance of any patient: families never pay for treatment not covered by insurance, and families without insurance are never asked to pay.

ARTIST PROFILE

In 2009, Laura Corlin graduated from The University of the Arts, the only university in the United States dedicated exclusively to the visual, performing, and media arts. She has continued her charitable work, performing at children's hospitals and organizing concerts with other University of the Arts students to raise money for hospitalized children. She intends to pursue a graduate degree in music therapy.

Laura Corlin
Photo by Pat Corlin

In 2003, she wrote:

I would like to share two special experiences from my very first hospital visit with you, and I hope you enjoy hearing it as much as I liked experiencing it. The first was with a very small and fragile little boy, much too small for his age. Before my performance he looked sad and lost in the endless halls of the hospital, but by the end this boy was smiling. He seemed as though he was anywhere but at the hospital.

The second experience is one that lasted far beyond the hospital visit. Justin, from Wisconsin, was feeling very ill, but he came out of his room to watch my performance anyway, lying with his head on his mother's lap. Although he could not lift his head, I watched as his feet were tapping to the music. After my performance, his mother asked me if I would follow her to the computer room where she proceeded to play a song that her husband had written for their son. As I listened to the song, my heart melted. I felt the joy and sadness they were feeling and when she asked me if I would record the song for them, I was more than willing. I recorded "Justin's Song" as soon as I got home. That Valentine's Day, Justin sent me a card and some candies thanking me for his song and for my kindness. I am so glad to say that Justin is now living at home with his family, recovered from his illness.

Laura's sister, Meagan, helped create and run the nonprofit Starmight Foundation, which inspires and supports youth volunteerism and promotes Laura's music-related projects.

Laura Corlin's recordings can be purchased at www.starmightfoundation.org and www.cdbaby.com.

"This program is dedicated to the memory of Charles Kennedy. Loving grandfather, noble serviceman, respected citizen of Burlington, MA, proud father and husband, and an inspiration to all who knew him. Papa, this program was inspired by you, and we live each day with you in our hearts and memories. We love and miss you."

– Starmight Foundation dedication

CONTACT INFORMATION

For information about contacting Laura Corlin, see Appendix A, page 215.

"You can look at disease as a form of disharmony. And there's no organ system in the body that's not affected by sound and music and vibration."

–Mitchell Gaynor, M.D.

Multi Image Matrix Wall – A multiple image display with a combination of matrix screens

Seewall

The Medical University of South Carolina Children's Hospital
Charleston, South Carolina

Vivid images of a virtual aquarium engage and soothe children, families, and visitors.

Seewall in MUSC Children's Hospital lobby

SEEWALL

The *Seewall* project at the Medical University of South Carolina Children's Hospital provides pediatric patients with beautiful and interesting distractions from their worries and their pain.

Designed by artists Olga Stamatiou and Matthew Zappia in conjunction with filmmaker Rocco Zappia, *Seewall* includes an 18-foot by eight-foot lobby display and a range of mobile units that can be deployed in different areas throughout the hospital. Moving images of fish and other sea life appear against a lush painted background. The lobby display is accompanied by classical music performed by the Charleston Symphony Orchestra. Live video and audio links with the South Carolina Aquarium allow children to watch and talk with divers who are in the aquarium's tank. Interactive features permit patients and other users to create art and play educational games.

As John Sanders, administrator of MUSC Children's Hospital, has said, "The *Seewall* is a pioneer in this arena, thus allowing us to best meet the needs of our vulnerable patients. As we expand the applications of the *Seewall*, we foresee additional future promise. The *Seewall* will function as a powerful adjunct in reducing pain and anxiety in children with both acute and chronic painful conditions."

Art-Making

Dance

Literary

Media

Music

Performance

Visual

Multi Image Matrix Wall – A high impact SEEWALL unit with multiple backlit images and LCD screens, including matrix, for a virtual aquarium effect

"When I got to the lobby I found not only a pediatric patient and his mom enjoying the art and music, but an adult patient who was completely relaxed by what he was seeing and hearing. Everyone is raving about it! Thank you for adding such beauty and peace to our lobby."

– Christine Messick, MUSC Children's Hospital Volunteer Program

A mobile unit can be placed anywhere needed.

Partner Institution

The Medical University of South Carolina Children's Hospital is one of three hospitals that make up the Medical University of South Carolina Medical Center. Overall, the Medical University of South Carolina also includes a college of medicine and five other colleges, which are devoted to nursing, pharmacy, health professions, dental science, and graduate studies.

Rocco Zappia, Olga Stamatiou, and
Matthew Zappia

ARTIST PROFILES

Olga Stamatiou, Rocco Zappia, and Matt Zappia are
officers of SEEWALL STUDIOS, and of SEEWALL CHILD
Foundation, a nonprofit company that provides *Seewall*
units at no charge to organizations that treat children
under stressful situations.

Ms. Stamatiou holds graduate degrees in fine arts and
art therapy. Her paintings have been shown widely in the
United States and Europe. Rocco Zappia has founded several innovative design and manufacturing companies and
participated in film production for major environmental
organizations, from New Orleans to the Arctic Circle. Matt
Zappia develops computer designs and animation for all
SEEWALL products along with the SEEWALL Aquafilms.

"Our goal with our SEEWALL CHILD nonprofit 501(c)(3)
is to provide SEEWALL displays, free of charge, to child-
oriented organizations with limited funds such as crisis
centers, orphanages, special-need centers, and
child-based relief organizations."

High-definition aquafilms create a virtual aquarium effect.

**"The Seewall looks
great! I have seen so
many kids, and adults/
employees, watching in
awe and interacting with
it. They are loving it and
us too."**

– Lisa McKellar, Manager, Pediatric Diagnostics
and Therapeutic Services Division of Pediatric
Cardiology

CONTACT INFORMATION

For information about contacting SEEWALL STUDIOS and SEEWALL CHILD,
see Appendix A, page 215.

"At the deepest level, the creative process and the healing process arise from a single source. When you are an artist, you are a healer; a wordless trust of the same mystery is the foundation of your work and its integrity."

– Rachel Naomi Remen, M.D.

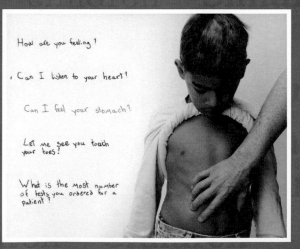

Page 1 with questions for doctors
Photo by Margot Geist

A Medical History for Doctors

The Children's Hospital
Aurora, Colorado

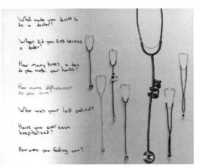

Page 2 with questions for doctors
Photo by Margot Geist

A young girl captures her medical experience with humor and wisdom.

Born with a complicated intestinal disorder, Anne Meyer-Miner spent a lot of her youth in doctors' offices and hospitals. When she was nine, she started asking questions of the medical professionals who were treating her, questions that broke down doctor-patient barriers and changed the mood in treatment rooms. As she explains:

> Sometimes when I'm in the hospital I don't know how to tell the nurse or doctor that I've answered the same question twelve times already, or that it hurts to lay on the metal table and roll from one side to the other. When I asked the doctors questions, I noticed they listened more to what I was thinking and feeling. I laughed and felt less scared when they answered the questions.

Meyer-Miner put together her questions, along with illustrations by her godmother Margot Geist, into a book they titled *A Medical History for Doctors*.

One physician said, "Her book showed me how even the youngest children use humor to fight back against the unpredictable nature of chronic disease, how humor can help them put bad situations into manageable perspective, and, most important, how humor can be a tool to promote civility and mutual respect between children and their doctors."

"It's best to express yourself.... Even though you are young, doctors need to listen to you." Anne Meyer-Miner says.

Art-Making

Dance

Literary

Media

Music

Performance

Visual

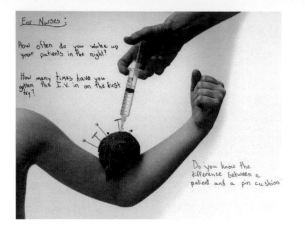

Page 3 with questions for nurses
Photo by Margot Geist

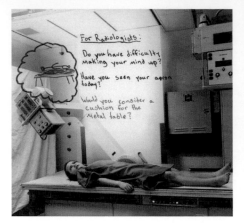

Page 4 with questions for radiologists
Photo by Margot Geist

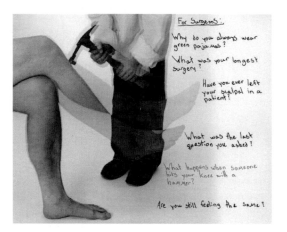

Page 6 with questions for surgeons
Photo by Margot Geist

"I still have the original copy of Anne's book on my desk and look at it often to remind myself not to get too self-important in my role as doctor... This sweet child in a few short printed pages absolutely nailed the foibles of her 'important' doctors and nurses by her quirky pictures and insightful commentary."

– Dr. Judith Sondheimer, Chief, Gastroenterology,
The Children's Hospital, Denver

Partner Institution

The Children's Hospital, in Aurora, Colorado, provides comprehensive care at a main campus and in 13 additional locations, with more than 1,000 pediatric specialists and more than 3,000 full-time employees. It has been ranked among the top ten pediatric care facilities by *US News & World Report* and *Parents Magazine*.

Anne Meyer-Miner
Photo by Margot Geist

ARTIST PROFILE

"I am always trying to find humor and look on the bright side of whatever I am doing. I think I tried to do this before I wrote *A Medical History for Doctors*, but now I can really see the effects of being positive and finding laughter in my life. Telling my story in this way has validated my experience. I am hoping patients, especially kids, will be able to laugh about what I have written and be inspired to find the humor around them even during a scary hospitalization."

ARTIST PROFILE

"I felt empowered to be able to turn the frustration I felt as a helpless onlooker of my goddaughter's medical experiences to one of making images that might improve the quality of the healthcare experience." – Margot Geist

Margot Geist

Anne, age 9, meets Patch Adams.
Photo by Margot Geist

"Patch Adams and I exchanged signed books at an awards ceremony. After returning home I received a letter from Patch saying he had read my manuscript and considered me a colleague. He also wrote, 'Let's go change the world.'"

CONTACT INFORMATION

For information about contacting Anne Meyer-Miner or Margot Geist, see Appendix A, page 215.

5

Projects Serving Cancer Patients

A *Music Rx*® staff member with a patient

Cancer patients often suffer from emotional distress and additional physical ailments that can interfere with their treatment and undermine their quality of life. Their family caregivers and other loved ones can also be subject to high levels of depression and stress-related syndromes.

For cancer patients, caregivers, and loved ones, creating art provides distractions from physical and psychological suffering, combats stress and depression, builds a sense of community and social support, and opens new pathways for important personal insights. Viewing art works created by other cancer patients can alleviate a sense of isolation and spark new perspectives.

Cancer centers throughout the world are incorporating arts therapies and arts programming into their services for inpatients and outpatients and using visual art to create a beautiful, nurturing environment.

"One day all the stress of coping with cancer hit me at once. I dropped onto the edge of my bed and felt my courage and energy desert me. Then I lifted my eyes to the paintings on my wall, the ones I had created in the painting group. There was my courage, inspiration, strength, and guidance shining back into me from the paintings. It was amazing – I felt lifted and renewed."
– A cancer patient

"Everybody needs beauty as well as bread, places to play in and pray in, where nature may heal and give strength to body and soul alike."

– John Muir

"Healing Touch"
Artist: Michele Angelo Petrone
© MAP Foundation

The Emotional Cancer Journey

The MAP Foundation
Sussex, England

An artist with cancer expresses his feelings and builds inspiring new pathways of communication for patients, loved ones, and medical professionals.

"The Journey"
Artist: Michele Angelo Petrone
© MAP Foundation

Diagnosed with Hodgkin's disease, a form of cancer, when he was thirty years old, Michele Angelo Petrone soon committed his considerable artistic talents, unstinting empathy, and personal vivacity to helping patients, their loved ones, and their caregivers better understand the emotional impacts of serious illness.

After multiple treatments for cancer, he succumbed to the disease at the age of 43, in 2007. In an obituary, the *Times* (London) wrote:

> In just 13 years he transformed attitudes towards people with life-threatening illness, enabling them to express their feelings through art in a way hitherto unheard of.

Petrone communicated his personal yet universal experiences through vivid paintings and eloquent words that were incorporated into a traveling exhibit and compiled into a book, *The Emotional Cancer Journey*. He also led scores of workshops to help others express their own feelings. Art and writings created by patients who participated in those workshops are collected in the book and exhibition, *Touching the Rainbow*, and works by healthcare professionals were presented in another exhibition, *Moving Pictures*.

The honesty, eloquence, and depth of Michele Petrone's painted and written expressions have helped many thousands of people in their struggles with cancer and other diseases.

Art-Making

Dance

Literary

Media

Music

Performance

Visual

A palliative care expert observed:

> Michele enabled people to break out from the limitation of language and express those feelings through a different medium.... Thanks to his vision, creativity, and understanding of the process, countless individuals found meaning, peace, and resolution....

A patient wrote:

> I found the paintings a true and wonderful example of the road one has to travel. The pain, the anger, the stress, and all the emotions of myself are there. I hope it helps other sufferers and their family and friends to cope as well.

Another said:

> I am moved by the transformative potential in our spirit, which can take such a difficult life experience and make it into something so powerful and so vividly beautiful.

For Michele Petrone, the importance of his work lay in the hearts, souls, and minds of those who chose to engage with their own experiences. "My aim was...to guide them so they felt free to express whatever they wanted," he wrote. "What was important was what each individual got out of it."

"So Much Love"
Artwork and quote by
Michele Angelo Petrone
© MAP Foundation

So much love

A serious illness does for your appetite for love what steroids do for your appetite for food. When feeling low and vulnerable, your appetite for love can become insatiable. Fortunately, love came to me from so many different sources, some friends, of course, from my lover – well that goes without saying, doesn't it. The nurses and counsellors and even the cleaners gave so much love. It means so much to me even now. Some of the doctors also expressed love. Is a doctor a better doctor if he (or she) is loving? Undoubtedly, no question of it.

Partner Institution

The MAP Foundation offers workshops for healthcare professionals based on the model created by Michele Petrone, provides loans of his exhibitions, and arranges lectures and presentations. It is located at the University of Sussex, within the Cancer Research UK Psychosocial Oncology Group.

ARTIST PROFILE

Michele Petrone
Photo by Lucinda Beatty

Born of Italian parents, Michele Angelo Petrone was trained as an artist in England and his early work was exhibited widely in solo and group shows. He served on the executive committee of the National Artists Association in the United Kingdom from 1991 to 1994.

He became artist-in-residence at several schools and cancer centers and taught in universities and hospitals. In 2002, he created the MAP Foundation to assure that his work would be sustained beyond his lifetime, and he indefatigably continued presenting his workshops until just a few weeks before his death.

Between night and day

As time goes by, night follows day, and day follows night – a natural cycle without beginning, without end and without gaps. Life's cycle continues without interruption, or at least it should. I found myself caught between life and death, light and dark, banished to an unknown place – between night and day. The illness forced itself into my life where there was no place for it. The arrival of illness stole a place and time that should have been destined for better things.

"Night and Day"
Artwork by Michele Angelo Petrone
© MAP Foundation

Michele Petrone's book, *The Emotional Cancer Journey*, can be purchased at www.mapfoundation.org

CONTACT INFORMATION

For information about contacting the MAP Foundation, see Appendix A, page 215.

"Beauty saves.
Beauty heals.
Beauty motivates.
Beauty unites.
Beauty returns us to our origins,
and here lies the ultimate act of
saving, of healing, of overcoming
dualism."

– Matthew Fox

Arts at the Bedside

Sylvester Comprehensive Cancer Center at
University of Miami Miller School of Medicine
Miami, Florida

Creating art reduces depression, stress, and anxiety among family caregivers of cancer patients.

A patient makes an art project with the "Art Kart" facilitator at South Miami Hospital.

In 2002, Sandra Walsh, who is now a professor in the School of Nursing at Barry University, created the *Arts at the Bedside* program at the Sylvester Comprehensive Cancer Center at the University of Miami Miller School of Medicine. It has been shown through research that the program decreased depression, reduced stress and anxiety, and increased positive emotions among those who participated in the study.

In the project, a trained staff person brought an "Art Kart" stocked with art supplies to areas of the hospital where patients and family caregivers were located – to inpatients' bedsides, for example, and to the outpatient chemotherapy center – and offered them an opportunity to try out a creative art project. Among the available activities were watercoloring, ceramics, wood painting, silk rubbings, wallhangings, and monoprint cards.

The activities offered a wide range of possible involvement. A monoprint might take only a minute or two to complete, while other activities could require more attention. The staff person possessed the skills to assist the participants with whatever activities they might wish to undertake.

Many people hesitated at first, saying things like, "I'm no artist." But after looking at the sample creations displayed at the Art Kart and receiving gentle encouragement from a staff person – along with reassurance that there was no cost for creating this art – many did join in.[1]

Art-Making

Dance

Literary

Media

Music

Performance

Visual

A teacher and students make images.

Reviewing her experience, Walsh observes, "*Arts at the Bedside* is contagious and I believe even necessary for the human spirit. One only has to look at the transformation on the faces of the people engaged in these activities to confirm this belief. Patients and students all around me are falling in love with art and art making."

An outpatient chemotherapy patient told researchers, "I have to come to the hospital for treatment twice a week and used to dread these visits. Now I think, 'Oh, today is my art day' – and I can't wait to get there." An inpatient who was scheduled to be discharged called her son and told him not to pick her up too early because she wanted to complete more art projects before she left the hospital. A nurse who had recently submitted her retirement papers exclaimed, "Where have you all been? I might just not retire after all!"

"This type of approach needs to be everywhere," another nurse said. "For nurses, for doctors, for patients – just everywhere. I don't know when I have felt so stress-free." Sandra Walsh is doing her best to see that bedside arts programs flourish wherever there is a need. Through her leadership, a program has been set in place at South Miami Hospital, and training in bedside art has been incorporated into a nursing-school curriculum in the United States and tested among nursing students in Taiwan.[2] The Sylvester Comprehensive Cancer Center continues to offer the program Walsh established to patients as an Arts in Medicine initiative, and has expanded it to a satellite facility, Sylvester at Deerfield Beach.

Partner Institution

Sylvester Comprehensive Cancer Center at the University of Miami Miller School of Medicine opened in 1992 to provide comprehensive cancer services and today serves as the hub for cancer-related research, diagnosis, and treatment at UHealth – the University of Miami Health System. Sylvester handles nearly 1,600 inpatient admissions annually, performs 2,700 surgical procedures, and treats more than 3,700 new cancer patients. All Sylvester physicians are on the faculty of the Miller School of Medicine, South Florida's only academic medical center. In addition, Sylvester physicians and scientists are engaged in more than 200 clinical trials and receive more than $36 million annually in research grants. Sylvester at Deerfield Beach opened in 2003 to better meet the needs of residents of Broward and Palm Beach counties.

Sandra Walsh

ARTIST PROFILE

Sandra Walsh, R.N., Ph.D., F.A.A.N. is a professor in the School of Nursing at Barry University in Miami Shores, Florida.

Arts at the Bedside evolved from her previous experiences using art to dramatically alter healthcare situations in which she found herself. In the 1990s, as a way of earning money while she worked toward her doctorate, she held down a job at an inpatient psychiatric facility for adolescents. Many of her patients had been admitted directly to the locked ward from an emergency room after a suicide attempt, or after being taken into custody by the police for threatening to harm others.

Caring toward her patients but worried about safety and frustrated by the difficulty she had in reaching them, she called upon a skill she had developed in her youth but largely set aside during her nursing career: she began sketching their portraits.

"The atmosphere on the unit changed almost immediately," Walsh says:

> Even the most hyperactive patients began to patiently wait their turns for a prized portrait. One said, "I never have had a photo of myself, and to have a real portrait, that is really something." Patients began to pose for long times with no mention of needing a break. Suddenly, and without effort, we were friends. We began to work on art projects together and I discovered that even suicidal teens could anticipate positive futures when they become engaged in making art.

Color is the keyboard, the eyes are the harmonies, the soul is the piano with many strings. The artist is the hand that plays, touching one key or another, to cause vibrations in the soul.

– Wassily Kandinsky

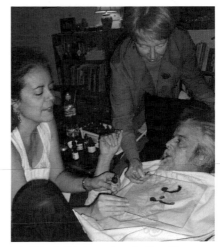

Patient Reggie Nicholson makes art with assistance from his wife, Carol, and Sandra Walsh (right).
Photo by Tom Moore

One of the key focal points of *Arts at the Bedside* – helping family members who were caring for cancer patients – grew in part from another profound personal experience Walsh had of the relationship between art and healing. Here's how she tells it:

My father became gravely ill and I found myself on an oncology unit at his bedside. To lessen my anxiety, I brought some pastels and pencils to the hospital and began to sketch. Dad suddenly said, "Draw me, you see I'm paralyzed, I'll be a great model." I was taken aback and asked, "With oxygen tubes and everything?" He said, "Yes – and in living color, please."

During those times when I was drawing, the relationship between my dad and I, once strained and distant, became close and comforting. The many portraits I created during his last days somehow helped me to forget and forgive him for his many absences from my life. I felt a sense of peace and acceptance between us. We filled his hospital room with portraits of his downhill trajectory. As his condition deteriorated, I noticed that I eventually changed from the use of color to black and white. He was proud and even curious about each image. When medical students, interns, and residents looked shocked and skeptical about the display of portraits, he proudly introduced me as "my daughter, the artist." He remained pleasant, alert, and even sweet – a side I seldom saw in him. It seemed we communicated in a positive way never before possible. It is interesting in retrospect that I returned to color in the last portrait, "Letting Go."[3]

CONTACT INFORMATION

For information about contacting Sandra Walsh, see Appendix A, page 215.

"Biscayne Bay Walk"
Artwork by Sandra Walsh

An accomplished artist herself, Walsh has won awards at the Miami Watercolor Society show. This work, "Biscayne Bay Walk," won the President's Award in 2008.

1. The artists and nurses who staffed Arts at The Bedside received training that increased their capacity to work effectively with those facing end-of-life issues. Among the sources of this training were Very Special Arts of Florida (www.vsafl.org), and awareness of the End-of-Life Model (see Hogan, N., Morse, J., and Tason, M.. "Toward an Experiential Theory of Bereavement" *Omega: Journal of Death and Dying*, 33(1): 43-65 (1996)

2. For more information, see Chen, S., and Walsh. S. "The Effect of a Creative-Bonding Intervention on Taiwanese Nursing Students' Self-Transcendence and Attitudes toward Elders." *Research in Nursing & Health*, 32(2): 204-209 (2009)

3. Dr. Walsh thanks her daughter, Lyn Taylor Hale, for assistance in preparing this description.

Patients Experiencing Cancer

"It is not sufficient to see and to know the beauty of a work. We must feel and be affected by it."

– Voltaire

Monoprint done by a patient

Projects Serving Cancer Patients

"Everything in
the universe
has rhythm.
Everything dances."

– Maya Angelou

A patient participates in the *Music Rx®* program

Music Rx®

Children's Cancer Association
Portland, Oregon

Music in many forms helps lighten the burden of serious illness for children and their families.

Music Rx® director interactes with a patient.

Knowing how music can relieve fear, anxiety, and even pain, how much of it, in how many forms, would you make available to children with cancer and their families? If the life of your own five-year-old child had been taken by cancer, how much might you do to alleviate the suffering of other children and their families?

In 1995, the same year that her daughter Alexandra succumbed to cancer, Regina Ellis joined with others to form the Children's Cancer Association (CCA) to begin answering those questions and others. CAA has grown from a small volunteer organization to having a paid staff of nineteen that enlists over nine hundred volunteers annually to bring more than twelve thousand service interactions to children and families. CCA's programs include resources such as its "Kids' Cancer Pages" and "Family Resource Guide"; a "Chemo Pal®" mentor program; a bilingual "LifeSupport Family Enrichment Program"; and "Caring Cabin™," a retreat home on the Oregon Coast.

CCA's *Music Rx®* program, which was initiated by Ellis and has been further developed by current program director Emily Hoffmann and former program director Karen Kurzawa, offers a variety of services to children and families at Portland-area hospitals and other medical facilities. Among the services made available are a mobile music cart library with hundreds of items, including rap machines, electronic drums, marimbas, harps, and iPods; one-on-one and group music activities; and hosted karaoke events.

Art-Making

Dance

Literary

Media

Music

Performance

Visual

Teresa (pictured above) was introduced to Soundbeam. She steered her wheelchair in front of the beams and her movements triggered the motion sensitive beams to register a sound wave. By sequencing with the keyboard's processor, the Soundbeam turned motion into music. *Music Rx®* allowed Teresa to independently conduct a jazz trio, an African safari, a bell choir, and a blues song despite her extreme mobility limitations.

In 2008, *Music Rx®* served over 2,300 children at 25 children's units. Its on-call music outreach program provided end-of-life comfort to over 550 terminally ill children and teens and their grieving families. Over 50 volunteers created more than 400 hours of live, soothing music throughout pediatric hallways.

Working with a team of outside evaluation consultants, *Music Rx®* designed and conducted surveys of patient families and medical professionals. Overall, 100 percent of medical professionals said they were "strongly satisfied" with the program's impact, and 100 percent of the family respondents said they were either "strongly satisfied" or "satisfied." Very positive reactions were also recorded from both groups regarding pain management, relaxation, and distraction.

A *Music Rx®* staff member with a patient

"This program enables people to reach children with neurological challenges (like my child) in ways you just wouldn't believe. He had fun for a few moments in a long hard day."

– A mother

Partner Institution

Legacy Emanuel Children's Hospital, in Portland, Oregon, is the Flagship Partner of the Children's Cancer Association. A full-service 155-bed hospital-within-a-hospital on the campus of Legacy Emanuel Hospital & Medical Center, it includes more than 60 pediatric medical and surgical specialists and 85 community pediatricians.

Doernbecher Children's Hospital, in Portland, is the Community Partner of the Children's Cancer Association. Affiliated with the Oregon Health & Science University, it has more than 1,300 doctors and staff engaged in diagnosing and treating both common illnesses and complex diseases.

CCA has two other Community Partners in Portland, *CARES Northwest* (a community-based medical program for the assessment, treatment, and prevention of child abuse) and *The Center for Medically Fragile Children at Providence Child Center* (the only nursing facility in the Northwest providing skilled care exclusively for children in a residential setting).

ARTIST PROFILE

Emily Hoffmann is national director of the *Music Rx*® Program for the Children's Cancer Association, leading a team of four staff and 50 volunteers in providing therapeutic music services to hospitalized children and their families. She also serves on the board of directors of the Oregon Association for Music Therapy.

The Music Rx® core team

"When seriously ill children and their families need more than medicine, CCA's innovative programs create joy one moment at a time."

— CCA mission statement

In 2008, *Music Rx®* unveiled its state-of-the-art Mobile Music Cart for Hospitalized Kids, which was designed in conjunction with Nike and Herman Miller.

The Mobile Music Cart

Music Rx® program brochure

In 2009, partnering with Starlight Children's Foundation, *Music Rx*® will expand its services to two California hospitals, Mattel Children's Hospital University of California Los Angeles and Miller Children's Hospital in Long Beach. For information about collaborating with *Music Rx*®, contact Emily Hoffmann.

CONTACT INFORMATION

For information about contacting Emily Hoffmann at Music Rx, see Appendix A, page 215.

"An artist is a dreamer consenting to dream of the actual world."

– George Santayana

A mural painted by *Art for Recovery* patients welcomes patients and visitors as they get off an elevator at an inpatient floor.
Photo by Karen Gehrman

The Firefly Project – Art for Recovery

University of California San Francisco Helen
Diller Family Comprehensive Cancer Center
San Francisco, California

**Patients, medical students,
and high school students
become "pen pals" and learn
about illness, wellness, and
the power of relationships.**

Fish Mural, a part of six different murals
painted by *Art for Recovery* staff and
patients on the ceilings of the ultrasound
suites *Photo by Karen Gehrman*

UCSF Helen Diller Family
Comprehensive
Cancer Center

In 1988, when Cynthia Perlis went to a San Francisco
hospital to learn more about the hospital's arts program
for elders, she was told that an oncologist at the University
of California San Francisco Medical Center at Mount Zion, Dr.
Ernest H. Rosenbaum, was interested in starting an expressive
arts program. When she met with Dr. Rosenbaum, she was
asked to become the director of *Art for Recovery*, and since
then she has built a broad and multifaceted program, now
based at the University of California San Francisco Helen Diller
Family Comprehensive Cancer Center. This program has served
tens of thousands of patients facing life-threatening illnesses.

The many programs that Perlis has implemented include
the following:

> *Patient-created artwork,* through which patients have
> created more than 1500 artworks at their bedsides (over
> 500 canvases created by patients, visitors, and staff are
> displayed in a permanent installation).

> *Writing, music, poetry, and art-making workshops,* through
> which hundreds of patients have explored and expressed
> their feelings about illness, wellness, and the journey of life.

> *Murals in the clinics,* in which eight murals painted by
> artists with assistance from patients provide peaceful and
> harmonious settings for patients and staff.

> *Breast cancer quilts,* through which patients and commu-
> nity members have created more than 70 quilts to raise
> breast cancer awareness and give women and their loved
> ones a voice.

Art-Making

Dance

Literary

Media

Music

Performance

Visual

Perlis also conceived *The Firefly Project*, in which cancer patients exchange hand-written letters and personal artwork with teenagers and medical students. The patients range in age from 17 to 80, and the students are drawn from diverse communities throughout the Bay Area. Each May a "Healing Service" is held, at which the correspondents meet each other in person for the first time.

During two public presentations after that meeting, the patients and their students read on stage from a script using their letters.

Perlis observes:

> The insights and emotional experiences shared in these exchanges provide extraordinary glimpses into the inner realities of illness and the anxieties and aspirations of young doctors and teenagers. It was clear since the beginning of this project that everyone, both patients and students, wanted the same things: to be connected, to be validated by understanding, empathic, and compassionate listeners, and to be loved.

> Watching the students and patients on stage in a dramatic reading is remarkable. The patients, some who are very ill, have their time in the spotlight sharing their dramatic stories. The students rise to the occasion, mature and thoughtful and compassionate as they read from the script with their pen-pal patient.

Questionnaires distributed to the participating patients and students have shown "an increase in connectedness with an extended community; a community beyond the hospital walls or one's immediate peer group."[1]

"*The Firefly Project* has given me the experiences of friendship, loss, growth, and healing – experiences I am eternally thankful for and will carry with me the rest of my life."

– A high school student

A *Firefly Project* invitation

Partner Institution

The University of California San Francisco Helen Diller Family Comprehensive Cancer Center is an interdisciplinary initiative that combines basic science, clinical research, epidemiology/cancer control, and patient care throughout the University of California San Francisco. The Center's mission is the discovery and evolution of new ideas and information about cancer, from the research to the clinical implementation phases of cancer control.

ARTIST PROFILE

Today, Cynthia Perlis heads the Ida & Joseph Friend Cancer Resource Center at UCSF, as well as continuing her role as director of *Art for Recovery*. The Cancer Resource Center supports wellness and the healing process by providing patients and their loved ones with information, emotional support, and community resources.

Cynthia Perlis
Photo by Jennifer Melnick – Olio Arts

"I love my work. Every day I feel blessed to work with amazing people, to meet courageous and brave adults coping with life-threatening illnesses, to watch patients create an image from the deepest place in their soul that expresses their feelings.

"My dad died when I was two years old and I think I have always had great empathy for those who were 'different.' I was the only kid I knew without an intact family, but my mom was strong and independent and easily served as both mother and father. She always believed in me and felt that I had a responsibility to share my artistic ability in some way when I grew up." – Cynthia Perlis

"I have saved every letter between patient and student since I created The Firefly Project in 1992.... A thirteen-year-old student was writing to a woman coping with breast cancer who was in her 70s. Their letters were very light and cheerful until the patient pen-pal found out that her student had been diagnosed with cancer himself. She was beside herself with sadness and didn't know what to do. Soon their letters were about chemotherapy and what to eat, about fatigue and hair loss. When they met at year end, their relationship was met with understanding. The patient died several years later; the student is alive and well and in his 30s."

Art for Recovery **has prepared an instructional manual for any institution wishing to replicate** *The Firefly Project*, **and has also created "The Portable Artist," a manual for patient-created art. They can be purchased by emailing Cynthia Perlis at cynthia.perlis@ucsfmedctr.org.**

CONTACT INFORMATION

For information about contacting Cynthia Perlis at Art for Recovery, see Appendix A, page 215.

---

1. Evaluation data were obtained through questionnaires sent to patients and students containing two identical lists of adjectives. Respondents were asked to circle all that applied to them while they were creating a communication, and then to indicate how they felt after they had created a communication. Perlis writes, "The findings supported the original objective of this project – an increase in connectedness with an extended community; a community beyond the hospital walls or one's immediate peer group. The project provided a vehicle for the participating patients to communicate their hopes and sorrows with a younger generation while the students in turn acquired skills in communicating empathetic compassion and their characteristic positive optimism regarding future tomorrows."

Projects Serving Cancer Patients Projects Serving Cancer Patients Projects Serving Cancer Patients Projects Serving Cancer Patients Projects Serving Cancer Patients Projects Serving Cancer Patients Projects Serving Cancer Patients Projects Serving Cancer Patients Projects Serving Cancer Patients Projects Serving Cancer Patients Projects Serving Cancer Patients Projects Serving Cancer Patients Projects Serving Cancer Patients Projects Serving Cancer Patients Projects Serving Cancer Patients Projects Serving Cancer Patients Projects Serving Cancer Patients Projects Serving Cancer Patients Projects Serving Cancer Patients Projects Serving Cancer Patients

"Art opens the closets,
airs out the cellars and attics.
It brings healing."

— Julia Cameron

"Ishmael"
Artist: Susan Wood Reider

Strange Gifts: Honoring the Journey

Thompson Cancer Survival Center ▪ Knoxville, Tennessee
Wellness Community of East Tennessee ▪ Knoxville, Tennessee
University of Tennessee Cancer Institute ▪ Memphis, Tennessee

An artist's own experience with cancer enriches her work and guides her in helping cancer patients and others on life's journey.

"Head and Heart (Glowing Peace)"
Artist: Susan Wood Reider

I was proud to call myself a working artist when I was diagnosed with breast cancer in 1998. The recommended treatment was harsh, the psychological and emotional recovery equally tough. I took the reality of the 'wake-up call' seriously and devoted myself to a spiritual overhaul. From the beginning, I saw this malignancy not as enemy, but as messenger, the proverbial wake-up call to change. For me this meant it was time to go inward, sift through and reassess everything that had led to this moment, these circumstances. My mission: to seek out and let go many negative habits of mind and body, and to affirm only those things which would contribute to a new spiritual focus for my life. It was over a year until I resumed a life in the studio and a gallery presence.

When Susan Wood Reider returned to her studio, it was to create *Strange Gifts: Honoring the Journey*, an evolving portfolio of works that she describes as "a visual memoir of my personal journey, and an homage to the journeys of family, friends, neighbors, and strangers." Each image that she creates features the rose, a symbol of unfolding mystery, strength, and beauty. Some pieces honor and celebrate specific individuals, while others depict what she calls "the mish-mash of a mystery tour navigating physical, psychological, and spiritual realms of meaning."

Exhibited at facilities that include the University of Tennessee Medical Center, The Wellness Community of East Tennessee, and Thompson Cancer Survival Center, Reider's art has served as a core element of programs for healthcare organizations

Art-Making

Dance

Literary

Media

Music

Performance

Visual

> "*Over Me (Good Show)* represents a tribute to the earthly and heavenly angels that watch over us, and a hopeful mantra about the process of making this project a reality!"
>
> – Susan Wood Reider

"Over Me (Good Show)"
Artist: Susan Wood Reider

and workshops benefiting cancer survivors. In some workshops, she teaches participants how to create artworks to aid in their own wellness journeys. Here is one participant's description of that experience:

> I vividly remember the calm feeling, mixed with joy. As my collage slowly came together, it surprised me how the paint and items seemed to place themselves exactly where they needed to be. And as I shared my experience and interpretation with the group, the piece revealed a theme I wasn't even aware of at the time of its creation.

The portfolio of work that Susan Wood Reider created has been received as both compelling and inspiring to cancer victims. In a survey of attendees at one exhibit, for example, 100 percent of them said they would recommend it to their friends and colleagues. She says, "Aside from the significant benefits of mining and documenting my own healing experience, I particularly enjoy the role of liaison among arts and healthcare organizations. The community-building fostered by the project promoted enduring cooperative relationships among artists and medical professionals, administrators, and staff."

Partner Institution

Thompson Cancer Survival Center, in Knoxville, Tennessee, provides a wide range of services to cancer patients. It is affiliated with Covenant Health.

The Wellness Community of East Tennessee, based in Knoxville, provides support services for people with cancer and for their loved ones.

The University of Tennessee Medical Center Cancer Institute, based in Knoxville, provides surgical and general oncology care, cancer research, and cancer education.

ARTIST PROFILE

"As an artist and a cancer survivor, I am privileged to express an enthusiastic 'thank you' to life through art. The universe has responded in kind."

"Celebrating the creative and spiritual foundations of healing, my goal is to engage and encourage fellow travelers, affirming their beauty and their struggles through the language of art. My hope is that patients and survivors, loved ones and healing communities will share a vision of renewal and optimism." – Susan Wood Reider

Susan Wood Reider

"Individual images take shape through layering of color and text, collage and assemblage. The process yields miniature worlds which are transparent and complex, surprising and familiar, serious and fun. Each work represents a little prayer of gratitude for the fullness of life, embracing the beautiful and the ridiculous, the tragic and the sublime."

"A Part (Dream Weaver)"
Artist: Susan Wood Reider

"A Part (Dream Weaver) is an attempt to picture displacement, transition and movement. We are each a collection of body parts held together by something intangible, our inner Self. Difficult passages sometimes part the way for necessary growth and positive transformation. This piece is dedicated to my sister, Ann."

—Susan Wood Reider

CONTACT INFORMATION

For information about contacting Susan Wood Reider, see Appendix A, page 215.

Projects Serving
Adolescents and Young Adults

Projects Serving
Adolescents and Young Adults

Projects Serving
Adolescents and Young Adults

Projects Serving
Adolescents and Young Adults

Projects Serving
Adolescents and Young Adults

Projects Serving
Adolescents and Young Adults

Projects Serving
Adolescents and Young Adults

Projects Serving
Adolescents and Young Adults

Projects Serving
Adolescents and Young Adults

Projects Serving
Adolescents and Young Adults

6
Projects Serving Adolescents and Young Adults

Cheryl Chapin, a long-time painter and *Arts Access* participant, explores a new painting style, assisted by Facilitator and Studio Manager Scott Beil. *Photo by Dave Scull*

Many projects described elsewhere in the book serve adolescents and young adults; the case examples in this chapter show particular ways in which the arts can help young adults to overcome physical, psychological, and emotional obstacles, aid others, and thrive.

"A boy and his father were walking along a road when they came across a large stone. The boy said to his father, 'Do you think if I use all my strength, I can move this rock?' His father answered, 'If you use all your strength, I'm sure you can do it.' The boy began to push the rock. Exerting himself as much as he could, he pushed and pushed. The rock did not move. Discouraged, he said to his father, 'You were wrong. I can't do it.' His father placed his arm around the boy's shoulder and said, 'No, son. You didn't use all your strength – you didn't ask me to help.'" – David J. Wolpe

"Creativity is the mother of all energies, nurturer of your most alive self. It charges up every part of you. When you're plugged in, a spontaneous combustion occurs that 'artists' don't have a monopoly on. This energy rises from your own life force and from a larger spiritual flow."

– Judith Orloff, M.D.

Nick, an *Arts Access* artist, tries his hand at painting, with stunning results.
Photo by Lyn Sanders

Arts Access

Matheny Medical and Educational Center
Peapack, New Jersey

Scott Beil (left) and Ryan Cornine (right) work on
a painting. *Photo by Lyn Sanders*

**Severely disabled
individuals express
their creativity, share it
with a broader community,
and enjoy fuller and
richer lives.**

These artists' bodies are frozen but their minds are volcanic.

That's how Lyn Sanders describes the severely disabled
individuals she has been working with since 1993 as they
express themselves through the visual, literary, musical, and
performing arts. The program Sanders now directs, *Arts
Access*, began as a pilot project with the Matheny Medical and
Educational Center in New Jersey. The visionary project was
driven by the interrelated goals of assisting severely disabled
individuals to live their lives fully and to have their creative
talents recognized and shared with the community at large.

Using systems and methodologies perfected over many
years that permit artists with severe disabilities to precisely
communicate their artistic intent, able-bodied artists facilitate
the participants' work, acting only as neutral conduits for
the participants' ideas. Independent research verifies that
each facilitator safeguards the creative integrity of each
participant's artistic process.

In the case of performances, dancers and actors precisely
execute the participants' creative visions, and the participants
themselves often choose to perform as well. A professional
ballet company facilitates the dance performances. One
observer of a performance wrote, "Dancer Shaleena To-
massini of Matheny might have been an angel with human
creativity and imagination when she danced with members of
the Roxey Ballet Company. Her wheelchair was nothing more

Art-Making
Dance
Literary
Media
Music
Performance
Visual

than a prop for the performance, which received a full minute's standing ovation at its stirring conclusion."

As one participant has said, "Every paint stroke, every word, every dance step is ours. Yes, you're our hands, but *Arts Access* is so much higher than even art. It's survival, it's being able to let out emotions, having a quiet place to run. A sanctuary. And if a piece of art comes out, so much the better."

Dance participant Chet Cheesman
Photo by Lyn Sanders

Brad Goldman paints.
Photo by Lyn Sanders

"**Now, after years of little more than existing, my son has a life; he has a passion unlike any that he has ever had, for at last he can actually do something instead of having it done for him. At last, he can communicate on his terms; he can communicate on a level that transcends any normal communication. He can express his emotions, his feelings, and even his opinions through his art. And because of this, his mind has begun to soar.**"

– Mother of an *Arts Access* participant

Partner Institution

Matheny Medical and Education Center, in Peapack, New Jersey, is a teaching hospital and facility for people of all ages with developmental disabilities, specializing in the care of children and adults with cerebral palsy, muscular dystrophy, spina bifida, and Lesch-Nyhan Disease. It was founded in 1946 by Walter and Marguerite Matheny, the parents of a child born with cerebral palsy, with three students and an operating budget of $3,000 obtained through a GI Loan.

ARTIST PROFILE

An accomplished photographer, Lyn Sanders has headed *Arts Access* since 1995. She recounts her first involvement with the program, just as it was beginning in 1993:

Arts Access staff: Keith Garletts, Scott Bell, Alex Stojko, Eileen Murray, Katina Ansen, Elaine Chong, Daniel Vallejo, and Lyn Sanders

"Like a magic carpet ride, the music and dance numbers transported the audience to places most of us had never visited. Many left the theater with a fuller sense of what it means to be human."

– School headmaster

The first day I walked through Matheny's sliding glass doors and inside the lobby, I was holding several cameras in my hands with several more slung over my shoulders. I was carrying too much and concentrating on not dropping anything. When I looked up and focused in on the lobby, a group of wheelchairs had gathered around me like a swarm of bees. I almost gasped aloud when I saw them. Heads hanging, arms twisted, huge smiles on some with crooked teeth. I truly did not know what to think, what to say, or how to act. This was a foreign land to me. I felt so uncomfortable that I wanted to bolt. I think the only solace for me at that moment was the realization that I had only two hours to go....

Although going to Matheny in those early days was sometimes hard, it was mostly remarkable and the students inspired and inspiring. They are fearless artists and sensitive human beings. Their honesty, their candor, their laughter and their tears were so real, real beyond that of any other person I have ever met. They were, because of or in spite of their very severe disabilities, more able to reach their artistic truth, their own realities, in a way that many able-bodied artists find hard to do.

An Arts Access participant summed it up best: "Art is in your head and heart, not in your hands."

CONTACT INFORMATION

For information about contacting Lyn Sanders at Arts Access, see Appendix A, page 215.

"I think I did not use medication to give birth because the group work gave me the strength to do without. I learned a lot about breathing and how to move into positions of comfort."

– Prenatal Therapeutic Dance participant

Graphic from flyer created by Patricia Schillaci inviting pregnant women to her movement class

Prenatal Therapeutic Dance Project

Settlement Health
New York, New York

Flyer created by Patricia Schillaci

Pregnant women who participate in dance classes are healthier, happier, and better-informed, and they bond better with their babies.

You are invited to...

Join with pregnant women and express yourself creatively. Relieve stress, exercise lightly, and learn how body awareness and movement aid in bonding and communicating with your baby.

Throughout 2007, Patricia Caballero Schillaci distributed fliers with that message, in English and Spanish, among patients at Settlement Health in New York City's East Harlem neighborhood. The patients of Settlement Health are part of a population that is often medically underserved, and many are at risk during their pregnancies as a result of issues that include poverty, stress, depression, domestic violence, and lack of extended-family support.

Women who accepted Schillaci's invitation attended 75-minute classes during which they participated in dance activities and expressed issues and themes related to their pregnancies through dance movements. Schillaci's program aimed to reduce the women's physical discomfort and improve their psychological states related to such issues as body image, self-esteem, and perception of support. The women were also able to communicate prenatal care information and improve their ability to cope with delivery and the associated hospital stay.

Schillaci's program succeeded. A survey conducted after the program had ended demonstrated the following outcomes, among others:

Art-Making

Dance

Literary

Media

Music

Performance

Visual

Participants explore expressive themes.

"I never knew I could move that way during pregnancy."

– program participant

100 percent of the respondents reported decreases in discomfort from stiffness and muscle tension;

100 percent reported increased energy levels;

100 percent reported increased pregnancy-care knowledge;

90 percent reported increased self-esteem;

90 percent reported that they connected better with their babies

While 60 percent of them said that they would have complied with their scheduled prenatal care medical visits without the program, the other 40 percent said that the program had given them additional encouragement that helped them comply with that schedule.

When they delivered their babies, all of the participants stayed three days or less in the hospital, with 40 percent attributing their quick recovery to participation in Schillaci's program.

Women are empowered for birth.

Partner Institution

Settlement Health is a nonprofit community health center that has served New York City's East Harlem neighborhood since 1977. Handling over 45,000 health care visits each year, Settlement Health also works collaboratively with area hospitals and other community resources.

Patricia Caballero Schillaci

ARTIST PROFILE

Patricia Caballero Schillaci became a doctoral candidate at Teachers College Columbia University in 2004, after more than 20 years of training and experience in dance and dance therapy. While she was a student in the doctoral program, she worked full-time as a perinatal health counselor at Settlement Health.

> "I experienced how dance and music are a universal way of bringing people together to discuss themes common to all. Although there are cultural differences in how we express ourselves both physically and emotionally, the women in the program were able to improve their level of physical comfort, self expression, and self esteem in unique and personal ways."

> "The most exhilarating aspect of the project was creating trust and unity in the group. It was wonderful to have women develop the trust to share a personal concern and use the group as a supportive entity." – Patricia Caballero Schillaci

"I feel like the group work allowed me to connect to my baby in a special way."

– program participant

Women warm up and come together.

CONTACT INFORMATION

For information about contacting Patricia Caballero Schillaci, see Appendix A, page 215.

Projects Serving
Adolescents and Young Adults
Projects Serving
Adolescents and Young Adults
Projects Serving
Adolescents and Young Adults

"In the depths of winter I finally learned there was in me an invincible summer."

– Albert Camus

A CADD resident experiences body casting and begins to understand boundaries which help with sensory integration issues.
Photo by Bradley Hospital Staff

Art as a Source of Healing

Emma Pendleton Bradley Hospital
East Providence, Rhode Island

Rhode Island School of Design and Brown University
Providence, Rhode Island

Everyone gains as art students and premed students help children and young adults with special needs create art.

"I don't want the projects. I want YOU!...
and I'll think of you whenever I fly mine.
Yes, always and forever."
Photo by Melinda M. Bridgman

Bradley Hospital
A Lifespan Partner

In many of the accounts presented in this book, artists and medical professionals whose careers are well advanced find ways to bring the healing power of art to people in need. At Rhode Island School of Design (RISD) and Brown University, college students are getting the same opportunity, at a considerably younger age.

Through a course called *Art as a Source of Healing*, the students design multi-media art projects as a catalyst for mentoring young patients from Bradley Hospital. The RISD students are undergraduate and graduate students. The Brown students are chosen mostly from its pre-med track. The patients are from Bradley's Center for Autism and Developmental Disabilities (CADD) and its Children's Residential and Family Treatment program (CRAFT). The CADD patients often have serious emotional and behavioral problems in addition to a developmental disability. The CRAFT patients are children between the ages of four and twelve who are participating in an intensive treatment regime to address emotional and behavioral issues before returning home to their families.

The RISD and Brown students spend at least two hours each week with their partners from Bradley. At the end of the semester the students each submit a "personal transformation project" that demonstrates visually, and in writing, how some aspect of the course has been healing to them. Their practicum project is designed to explore their mentoring relationship with their partner.

Art-Making
Dance
Literary
Media
Music
Performance
Visual

Performing arts as well as visual arts are incorporated into the program, and Bradley clinical staff participate in teaching, mentoring, and supporting the students who participate in the program as well as the young patients. Melinda M. Bridgman, the RISD faculty member who initiated the course together with fellow artist Ana Flores in 2000, still leads it today. "By involving the staff in the creative projects along with the patients," she observes, "their understanding of art and its potential to transform and heal is deepened."

The students' enthusiasm shines throughout the comments they add to their schools' mandatory course evaluations: "This course did a wonderful job at opening the connection between art and healing. As someone going to medical school shortly, this alternative look at healing and thought was superb." "It has definitely changed my view toward art and life." "It has truly opened my eyes to a new way of thinking and seeing about art and about people and life. It was such a valuable experience that could never have been learned from a textbook."

Or, as one student put it: *"Simply spectacular!"*

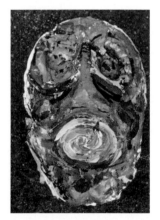

A papier mache mask created by one of the CADD residents, with the assistance of his mentor, to wear with his Halloween costume
Photo by Melinda M. Bridgman

"Jimmy was positive, encouraging, silly, able to laugh at himself, pretty focused and just sort of fun to be around and work with. I felt really comfortable working with him, and being myself, and helping him and answering questions and just the whole thing felt really great.... I did not view Jimmy as abnormal or hospitalized or anything; rather, through the course of the semester I have, in a lot of ways, felt Jimmy was more normal than most."

– A RISD student mentor

Partner Institution

Founded in 1931, Bradley Hospital was the nation's first psychiatric hospital devoted exclusively to children and adolescents. It is a teaching hospital affiliated with The Warren Alpert Medical School of Brown University and is a national center for training and research in child and adolescent psychiatry. It operates the Bradley School, a fully certified special education school.

Rhode Island School of Design (RISD), founded in 1877, is a private art and design college in Providence, Rhode Island, that offers undergraduate and graduate degree programs in 18 disciplines.

Brown University, founded in 1764, serves more than 7,500 students in its undergraduate, graduate, and medical-school programs in Providence, Rhode Island.

ARTIST PROFILE

A faculty member at Rhode Island School of Design, Melinda M. Bridgman co-conceived the *Art as a Source of Healing* course. She has been teaching it since the year 2000.

"I always wanted to be an artist and a nurse. My career search has been to find a way to do both. My mother was a professional artist. I spent many of my early years in her studio or outside with her sketching and painting. She was also a pianist. I would lie under the piano mesmerized by the music surrounding me as I watched her feet go up and down on the pedals. I loved taking care of family members when they were sick and needed special attention. Each summer during high school I worked as a volunteer in the local hospital." – Melinda Bridgman

Melinda Bridgman works with a student. *Photo by Jim Goodwin*

"The college that I attended had a first-rate art department and very well-respected nursing program. I tried to do both, but the requirements in each field were too stringent. I concentrated on fine arts, particularly jewelry design and silversmithing. I was fascinated with the alchemic possibility of turning base metals into gold. After graduating from college and continuing studies for an advanced degree in this field, I became involved with Connecticut Hospice, the first hospice in the United States. Being part of an interdisciplinary team that cared for all aspects of the patient brought together my interests in art and healthcare. While working with patients, family members, and staff my fascination with alchemy slowly began to transform into the possibility of turning illness into health."

CONTACT INFORMATION

For information about contacting Melinda M. Bridgman, see Appendix A, page 215.

"The children at Bradley Hospital are some of the most psychiatrically complex children you will find anywhere... The two hours that they spend with the RISD/Brown students are as beneficial and therapeutic as any other therapy that they receive during the week."

– Margaret Pacclone-Dyszlewski, Ph.D., Child and Adolescent Services, Bradley Hospital, and Clinical Assistant Professor, Warren Alpert Medical School, Brown University.

A student and a patient work on a project. *Photo by Robert W. Baker*

7 Projects Serving Seniors

Songwriting Works at the Jewish Home,
Mollie in CD production class.
Photo by Michael Wickler

Feelings of isolation, vulnerability, and frailty are among the challenges that can compound illness for older people. The case examples in this chapter show many ways in which a variety of arts modalities can address those feelings. Moreover, several show how the arts can help elders to maintain physical, mental, and emotional vitality.

"Research suggests that active participation in the arts and learning promotes physical health and enhances a sense of wellbeing among older adults; improves quality of life for those who are ill; and reduces the risk factors that lead to the need for long-term care."
— The Society for the Arts in Healthcare

"Art seems to me to be a state of soul more than anything else."

– Marc Chagall

Vera Dufault and staff from Crossroads Inlet Center Hospice in front of her "swarm" of dragonflies
Photo by Christine Graf

Dragonflies of Hope

Crossroads Inlet Center Hospice
Port Moody, British Columbia, Canada

Vera Dufault in front of her
"swarm" of dragonflies
Photo by Christine Graf

A hospice patient's artistic idea galvanizes an entire community and uplifts her final days.

Suffering from terminal cancer, Vera Dufault entered the Crossroads Inlet Center Hospice in Port Moody, British Columbia on January 23, 2005. That day, she joined other patients, family members, and staff in the "Art in the GreatRoom" activity that had been initiated by Linda Thiessen, president of B.C. Artists in Healthcare Society.

The hospice's logo bears a dragonfly, and Dufault assembled a charming pop-up dragonfly card and then created a pattern so others could make cards of their own.

So lovely and distinctive were the cards that Thiessen and the hospice's manager, Linda Kozina, decided to initiate a competition for the most beautiful dragonfly. Named *"Dragonflies of Hope,"* the competition would be judged by Vera Dufault.

As Dufault's health began to fail, the competition was accelerated. Thiessen approached the principal of a local elementary school and within 72 hours the students had colored 360 dragonflies and entered them in the competition.

Although she was very weak and confined to bed, on the first day of the judging, Vera Dufault held every dragonfly and examined it before giving directions about where it should be placed on the wall outside her room "so that everyone can see it." On the second day she asked the nursing staff to help her into a wheelchair. Dressed in a colorful gown, she supervised the installation of all the hundreds of dragonflies.

Art-Making

Dance

Literary

Media

Music

Performance

Visual

B.C. Artists in Healthcare Society has published a ten-volume manual, *Artcare Connections*. More information is available at http://artcare.1stfreehosting.com/publications.html

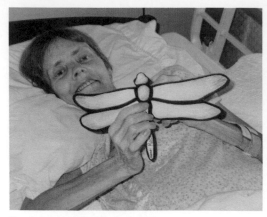

Vera Dufault holds her favorite dragonfly.
Photo by Christine Graf

The nearby city of Port Coquitlam invited Dufault to its May Day celebration, and dragonfly entries were requested from local schools and through local media. For six weeks she worked steadily to review all the dragonflies that had been submitted in her honor – a total of more than 4,500. She passed away on March 30.

"Through this project, Vera transformed right before our eyes," says hospice manager Linda Kozina. "Our belief is that we can put life into days, not days into life. Vera was profoundly empowered by this opportunity to give new meaning to her remaining days – and we all were changed by it."

A young visitor makes a dragonfly.
Photo by Christine Graf

"At first I was a little scared to see Vera because she was dying, but once I met her I felt happy because she was so happy. I think the dragonflies gave her a reason to live longer."

– Fifth-grade student

Partner Institution

Crossroads Inlet Center Hospice, located in Port Moody, British Columbia, is a freestanding ten-bed facility that opened in 2003. The Crossroads Hospice Society was formed in 1998 and engaged in years of challenging lobbying and fundraising in order to bring the hospice into being.

ARTIST PROFILE

Linda Thiessen is president of B.C. Artists in Healthcare Society, British Columbia's first artist-in-residence program. The organization, based in Port Coquitlam, has over 100 members providing programs in regional hospices, community, and cancer-care settings.

Linda Thiessen
Photo by Christine Graf

"In 2003, I graduated with a degree in fine arts, celebrated my fiftieth birthday, and fractured my foot! While waiting for X-ray results I read an article about the arts in healthcare in a local magazine – 'Creative Hearts Are Better Than Drugs.' It changed my life and inspired our ArtCare program." – Linda Thiessen

"I became involved with Linda Thiessen when she swept into my office, full of vim and enthusiasm. Linda offered to start the program without seed money. The beauty of the idea was its simplicity and it was thrilling to me to see how quickly the program was embraced by the entire team, families, and patients – and funders."
– Hospice manager Linda Kozina

CONTACT INFORMATION

For information about contacting Linda Thiessen at B.C. Artists in Healthcare Society, see Appendix A, page 215.

"I work here at hospice. Today I had the opportunity to drop everything I was doing and thinking...to color!" – Florice, hospice nursing team
Photo by Christine Graf

The first participants in the project, students at Castle Park Elementary School, color dragonflies. *Photo by Christine Graf*

"You hear an old song and the face of a lost loved one suddenly appears, and in the space of the song the loved one grabs your loneliness by the collar and throws it out the door."

– Graziano Marcheschi

The board game *Making Memories Together*.

Making Memories Together

Center on Aging, Health & Humanities at
The George Washington University
Washington, D.C.

**Alzheimer's patients
and their visitors revive
memories through a
unique board game.**

Gene Cohen's mother plays *Making Memories Together* with her granddaughter, Eliana.

Gene Cohen, a medical doctor who also holds a Ph.D. in gerontology, has been thinking for several decades about creativity in older people. Since 1994, he has headed the Center on Aging, Health & Humanities at The George Washington University.

When his father developed Alzheimer's disease in 1990, followed by his mother developing multi-infarct dementia in 2000, Cohen's career interests intersected with his personal experience. He responded resourcefully, creating two products, each aimed at the devastating effects of memory loss: not only does the affected person lose his or her ability to communicate effectively, but that very quality pains visitors and can deter further visits.

Cohen developed a noncompetitive board game, *Making Memories Together*, in which a beanbag is moved along a board that consists of squares denoting four different categories: people, animals, special occasions, and favorite objects. At each square, a "memory card" corresponding to the category is drawn and discussed. The memory cards use photographs, data, and recollections related to the life of the Alzheimer's patient.

Cohen provides this moving example of the impact the cards can have:

> During one of my mother's visits to my father, he did not recognize her, despite their having been married for more than fifty years. My mother was in tears. I then placed a short sequence of the memory cards on the table, showing pictures of my mother while my dad was in the navy courting her. He looked at the cards, then at my mother, then at the cards again, and back to my mother. All of a sudden, recognition came to him and he exclaimed, "Oh, the love of my life!"

Art-Making

Dance

Literary

Media

Music

Performance

Visual

The second product that Cohen pioneered for Alzheimer's patients was a video recording approach to combine images from the past with contemporary narration. Here's how he describes the technique:

> My dad had a scrapbook of photos and news clippings from his days in the navy. One was a newspaper clipping of a picture of my father where the navy featured him as a model sailor in recruiting other sailors. Another of the clippings was a newspaper article about the ship he sailed on. I took the video camera, zoomed in just on the ship so that the newspaper text was not seen, then gently rocked the camera to make it look as if the ship was sailing at sea, sound-injected "Anchors Aweigh," and then further zoomed in on the windows of the ship commenting, "I am looking for Ben Cohen on the U.S.S. Indianapolis."

"Watching this sequence on the video made my father all smiles," Cohen says.

Research studies of Cohen's board game and his video technique showed them to have "marked superiority over a visit as usual and various control conditions in terms of mood, engagement, and interest level on the part of the AD sufferer and level of satisfaction on the part of the significant other."

The board game, *Making Memories Together*, and other games developed by Cohen, are available for purchase at www.genco-games.com.

Gene Cohen and his mother play the *Making Memories Together* game. She is holding a memory card of her first great-grandchild, Ruby. When asked what it was like to be holding her new great-granddaughter, she exclaimed, "It was thrilling!"

Partner Institution

Founded in 1994, the Center on Aging, Health & Humanities at The George Washington University stimulates, coordinates, and conducts sponsored research on both the problems and potentials of aging, with the goal of improving the quality of life for older adults and their families. It is located in the George Washington University Medical Center, with interdisciplinary partnerships throughout the university. Particular attention is paid to understanding and tapping creative potential in later life and to creative problem-solving for social and health challenges associated with aging.

ARTIST PROFILE

Gene Cohen

Gene Cohen began to study aging more than 35 years ago during his training as a psychiatrist, when he was assigned to a rotation in a public housing project for older adults. He has written more than 150 publications on the subject of aging. His books include *The Creative Age: Awakening Human Potential in the Second Half of Life*, which was the first work wholly focused on creativity and aging, and *The Mature Mind: The Positive Power of the Aging Brain*. He also co-founded the Creativity Discovery Corps, whose mission is to identify and preserve the creative accomplishments and rich histories of under-recognized talented older adults.

> "In the end, when the Alzheimer's disease victims died, the families were left with two poignant exit gifts – biographies in the form of a video and a game, facilitated by their loved one who could no longer tell their story."

Photo side of a memory card of Gene Cohen's father, Ben Cohen

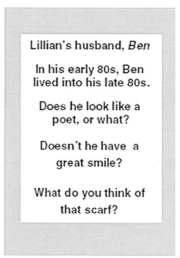

Lillian's husband, *Ben*

In his early 80s, Ben lived into his late 80s.

Does he look like a poet, or what?

Doesn't he have a great smile?

What do you think of that scarf?

Text side of a memory card of Gene Cohen's father, Ben Cohen

On November 7, 2009, while this book was in the final stages of printing, Dr. Gene Cohen died after a 14-year battle with cancer. A visionary, a leader, a scholar, an advocate, and an innovator, he was compassionate and generous to all who sought his help or guidance. As we worked with him to prepare this part of the book, he provided a quotation from Thomas Campbell to explain the significance of the products he had created. It is a quotation that we now apply to express our feelings about his passing:

"To live in the hearts we leave behind is not to die."

"The best review I ever got was not from a music critic, but from my father. He was 94 years old at the time and completely blind. He attended a Master Class I gave in London and sat there in his wheelchair for about three hours. When it was over, I went to speak with him. He lifted up his finger in his characteristic way and said, 'I see that you are actually a member of the healing profession.' It seemed to me the highest accolade."

– Orchestra conductor Benjamin Zander

Songwriting Works at the Jewish Home

Jewish Home of San Francisco
San Francisco, California

Composing music and performing enlivens elders, fights depression, educates staff and others, and gratifies families.

Jewish Home Singers and Songwriters perform "I'm 100 years old." *Photo by Gary Wagner*

"**W**hat do you like about Purim?" Judith-Kate Friedman asks a group of elders who reside at the skilled nursing facility, Jewish Home of San Francisco. The question is greeted by a rush of answers as the residents, whose average age is 87, recall events and characters from one of their favorite holidays.

Within an hour, the answers to that question and others have been transformed into the beginnings of a song. Its first verse goes,

> Life is like Purim.
> Sometimes a masquerade,
> Sometimes a party,
> Sometimes we are afraid.

And its chorus explains,

> Haman was a greedy man, an enemy, a louse.
> He wanted to kill the Jews in every house.

In subsequent sessions led by Friedman, these residents and other residents who join them will complete the song. One day they, or others, might perform it as part of the repertoire of nearly 100 songs that they and their peers have created. They might sing it to their fellow residents, or they might perform it for school children, college students, or at a community concert or national conference. They might even record it on a retail CD: One such CD, "Island on a Hill," has already been recorded and released.

A large proportion of the residents who create and sing these songs have early-stage Alzheimer's disease or other forms of

Art-Making
Dance
Literary
Media
Music
Performance
Visual

dementia. Fifty percent of the residents of Jewish Home of San Francisco are taking antidepressant medication; over 80 percent of them use wheelchairs or walkers. The facility's medical director, Dr. Jay Luxenberg, observes some of the many positive effects of participation in Friedman's program:

Jewish Home Psalms, Songs & Stories group performs their original songs at the dedication of their new synagogue, Congregation L'dor V'dor (from generation to generation).
Photo by Alain McLaughlin

Judith-Kate's program has resulted in quite dramatic improvement in depressive symptoms such as isolation, tearfulness, and poor appetite. I am also convinced that it has helped stave off depression in individuals who are at very high risk. I also find that participation in this program leads to increased interest in self-appearance (in part due to the residents performing) and better energy level and participation in other, related activities. Better appetite leads to better nutrition and ability to fight off infection. Better energy levels leads to more exercise tolerance, and then to improved strength, balance, and mobility.

All that might be quite enough to make this program extraordinarily valuable, but it is not all. Dr. Luxenberg continues:

I have heard staff comment how watching and listening to our residents be creative has increased their empathy toward the residents.... They also are amazed that residents with relatively severe dementia can still rally function to participate in the program.... Families get great pleasure from their loved ones' accomplishments, and I note that the process particularly excites the great-grandchildren.... The joy that pervades this program is evident to the young and to the young at heart.

Studying the program for a chapter she contributed to *The Oxford Handbook of Medical Ethnomusicology*, Dr. Theresa Allison observed its breadth and its impact:

They compose songs about relationships, vacations to Hawaii, love affairs, food, and faith. They discuss the central role of chicken soup in the Beat poem "Jewish Penicillin," and pass on their heritage through the instructions of "Recipe" and the accompanying song. "Gefilte Fish." These men and women escape the confines of wheelchairs and impaired memories by creating things that are new and which capture their knowledge and experience. For an hour at a time they can stop being "residents" and become students, tune-writers, and poets. As one songwriter says, "It's lifelong learning, all the time." [1]

Partner Institution

The Jewish Home of San Francisco began in 1871 as a residential center for twelve seniors and now has grown to a nine-acre comprehensive senior care center with five distinct buildings, serving more than 420 residents with diverse care needs and providing rehabilitation services to numerous others seeking short-term care. Almost 600 active volunteers contribute approximately 30,000 hours annually.

Judith-Kate Friedman
Photo by Alain McLaughlin

ARTIST PROFILE

Judith-Kate Friedman, who founded *Songwriting Works*™ in 1997, is an acclaimed vocalist, composer, recording artist, and producer. She won the 2007 "MindAlert" award from the MetLife Foundation/American Society on Aging, for her innovative programs enhancing mental fitness for older adults. In 2009, Songwriting Works received a grant from the National Endowment for the Arts to replicate its programs in the state of Washington.

At the Jewish Home, she enjoys strong support and collaboration from the facility's chaplain, Rabbi Sheldon Marder, and from Mark Friedlander, Director of Resident Programs.

"It has been a truly amazing phenomenon to witness the individual and collective talents of our elders as they come together in song... Our songwriting programs developed and inspired by Ms. Friedman are living proof that creativity never fades as we age and the power of song is alive in each and every one of us."
– Mark Friedlander

"My involvement in this program has been one of the most gratifying pastoral experiences of my thirty years in the rabbinate. The goal of the program is to help elders attain what Rabbi Abraham Joshua Heschel called 'a sense of significant being' through a combination of intellectual and spiritual exploration... I have been challenged to grow as a teacher and rabbi; I have been challenged to grow as a co-facilitator and collaborator; and I have been challenged, personally, in terms of my own beliefs."
– Rabbi Sheldon Marder

Birdie sings in "A Specially Wonderful Affair." *Photo from the film "A Specially Wonderful Affair" www.fdigital.net*

"Don't just ask what the world needs. Ask what makes you come alive and then go and do it, because what the world needs is people who have come alive."

—Howard Thurman

In an article about her work, Judith-Kate Friedman wrote:

> The voice is humanity's original instrument. Everyone has a song to sing. The ability to compose music and share one's song comes as freely to children as it does to birds.... Creativity and musicality persist as we age. Those who have had the pleasure of singing with elders discover that favorite songs can enliven them and open treasure troves of memories.... [T]hese benefits...increase when the songs they sing are their own.
>
> It is an honor to work so closely with, and be a student of, elders who, perhaps unwittingly, are such fine teachers. The artist's task is to learn by their example about living in each moment, to listen and help create opportunities for meaningful collaboration, and to remember the value of kindness – and music – in the preciousness of each day.[2]

CONTACT INFORMATION

For information about contacting Judith-Kate Friedman, see Appendix A, page 215.

A 30-minute documentary film, "A Specially Wonderful Affair," follows elders from the Jewish Home of San Francisco as they compose and perform their original songs. An excerpt can be seen, and the video can be purchased, at www.fdigital.net.

Jewish Home Psalms, Songs & Stories group elders perform their original songs at the dedication of their new synagogue.
Photo by Alain McLaughlin

Jewish Home participants perform at Art of Aging.
Photo by Gary Wagner

The music CD, "Island on a Hill," can be heard and purchased at www.cdbaby.com.

1. Allison, Theresa, "Songwriting in the Nursing Home: Transforming Institutionalization through Music," in Benjamin Koen, ed., *The Oxford Handbook of Medical Ethnomusicology* (New York: Oxford University Press, 2008)

2. Friedman, Judith-Kate. "Freeing the Voice Within: the Healing Art of Songwriting with Elders Diagnosed with Alzheimer's Disease and other Cognitive Disorders." *Signpost: Journal of Dementia and Mental Health Care for Older People* (Wales, UK: Spring, 2004); reprinted as "Freeing the Voice Within: the Healing Art of Songwriting," in *Aging Today* (November/December, 2004).

"I don't know what your destiny will be, but one thing I do know: the only ones among you who will be really happy are those who have sought and found how to serve."

– Albert Schweitzer

Singers at the Jewish Home
Photo by Michael Wickler

who knows if the moon's
a balloon, coming out of a keen city
in the sky – filled with pretty people?
(and if you and i should
get into it, if they
should take me and take you into their balloon,
why then
we'd go up higher with all the pretty people
than houses and steeples and clouds:
go sailing
away and away sailing into a keen
city which nobody's ever visited, where
always
    it's
     Spring) and everyone's
in love and flowers pick themselves

– e.e. cummings

IMAPers interpretation of e.e. cummings' "who knows if
the moon's a balloon"

Danceworks Intergenerational Multi-Arts Project: "Soul Shoes"

Aurora Adult Day Center
Milwaukee, Wisconsin

"Soul Shoes" Installation: Milwaukee Art Museum (250+ shoes painted by pairings of youth and elders) *Photo by Danceworks, Inc.*

Youngsters and elders create art, happiness, and understanding.

Danceworks
INCORPORATED
PERFORMANCE CLASSES OUTREACH

Start with 109 lonely and isolated elders in adult day care, the oldest of whom is 103 and more than half of whom suffer from a cognitive impairment such as Alzheimer's disease.

Add 116 boisterous sixth-graders from a diverse urban public school.

Put them together and what do you get? Among other things, you get the 2006 art exhibit *"Soul Shoes,"* in which pairs of children and elders decorated shoes, told stories about them, and created public dance performances to celebrate their creations.

You also get entirely new levels of understanding, empathy, and energy. Research on the project, combining observation and instrumentation, showed that the positive flow of energy increased exponentially when the older adults and youth came together for dance, art-making, interviews, and socialization, according to Deborah Farris, executive director of Milwaukee-based Danceworks, which led the project as part of its *Intergenerational Multi-Arts Project* (IMAP).

"There is a total transformation of energy. The environment becomes electric," says Danceworks' community programs director Janet Lew Carr. The elder participants in *"Soul Shoes"* also demonstrated new movement and visual arts skills, and their overall participation in activities at the adult day care center increased significantly. The day care center's manager, Mollie Bartelt, asserts, "We feel strongly that IMAP increases the overall quality of life of our participants, connects them with the community, and is a great success."

Art-Making
Dance
Literary
Media
Music
Performance
Visual

"Soul Shoes" was presented and performed in a variety of central Milwaukee institutions, including the Milwaukee Art Museum and the Cabot Theatre.

A student and a senior with dementia show off their creation.
Photo by Danceworks, Inc.

A student assists an elder who is blind.
Photo by Natalie Haefele.

A "soul shoe" takes form.
Photo by Danceworks, Inc.

"There were a handful of daycare clients, especially me, that only joined the dance sessions when the kids were present. The senior adults seemed to take very seriously their roles as partners, mentors, adopted grandparents, friends, etc. As much as they didn't want to miss out on the excitement of the intergenerational sessions, they didn't want to disappoint their young partners."

Partner Institution

Danceworks was founded in 1992. "Soul Shoes" was one project carried out by the Intergenerational Multi-Arts Project, which invites children and elders to explore their communities, life histories, and interpersonal connections through a variety of creative mediums, including dance, visual arts, writing, and music. Throughout the school year, the staff works with students and elders separately and jointly to build a curriculum of trust, investigation, and expression.

Aurora Adult Day Center is part of Aurora Healthcare, which has sites in more than 90 communities throughout eastern Wisconsin, including 13 hospitals, more than 100 clinics, and over 130 community pharmacies.

ARTIST PROFILE

Deborah Farris is executive director of Danceworks. She has served on dance and theatre faculties at Tulane University, the University of North Carolina, and the University of Wisconsin-Milwaukee. As an equity actress and dancer, she has performed extensively throughout the United States.

Deborah Farris

"Art is the one last experience that levels the playing field and that can provide a shared language, a moment, an inspiration point, an awakening. It's the creative impulse in each person that establishes their own unique individual place, importance, and value in society as a precious creation."

"An organization must be creative about applying an art form in new ways. Risk is essential to tackling everyday life. It's the risks in relationships, work, and life where you find your true spirit."

Janet Lew Carr

Janet Lew Carr is community programs director and gallery curator at Danceworks. She designs residencies, workshops, community events, and presentations for small groups as well as entire schools and organizations. She is a board certified and registered art therapist and registered nurse, active on the state and national levels of the American Art Therapy Association, and an adjunct faculty and intern supervisor at Mount Mary College art therapy graduate department.

> "We integrate the tools of the arts to touch as many individuals as we can. IMAP honors the interdependence of everyone involved in a magnificent creative and healing process to validate each person's gifts and talents. Its working framework addresses each individual's developmental tasks and needs, and reframes real life stories into living legacies colored with simple yet profound meaning."

CONTACT INFORMATION

For information about contacting Danceworks, see Appendix A, page 215.

Students and seniors from all IMAP schools and senior sites join together in interpretive movement at the Milwaukee Art Museum. *Photo by Danceworks, Inc.*

A ten-minute video about Danceworks and IMAP can be viewed at www.youtube.com/danceworks1661.

"Passion is in all great searches and is necessary to all creative endeavors."

– W. Eugene Smith

Chamira Jones presents Melvin Larson with his "memory box."
Photo by Satoru Takahashi

Memory Box and Days Forgotten

Turner Senior Resource Center, University of Michigan Geriatrics Center
Ann Arbor, Michigan

An art student's assignment to work with a dementia patient becomes a book and an enduring friendship.

Melvin Larson during a regular
Sunday visit by Chamira Jones
Photo by Chamira Jones

hamira**studios**

While she was an undergraduate studying at the University of Michigan School of Art and Design, Chamira Jones met 79-year-old Melvin Larson through an outreach course sponsored by the Turner Senior Resource Center in Ann Arbor. Larson suffered from dementia and Parkinson's disease. Jones's class assignment was to work with Larson, his family, medical staff, and caregivers, to create an art piece based on his life.

Jones and the other students in the course created "memory boxes" for their elder counterparts, and those art works were included in an exhibit on the college campus before they were returned permanently to the seniors.

Jones chose to maintain her friendship with Larson and his wife, visiting them regularly. She says:

> All through our relationship, Melvin had always spoken of his passion for writing with a mixture of wistfulness and bitterness, due largely to the fact that he had so much to say but virtually no audience. During our visits, he would let me sample from the large box of poetry that he had written over the decades, pride shining in his eyes as he watched me read them for the first time.

She decided to help him find an audience. As her senior thesis project, she found a publisher and created a book, *Days Forgotten: Poems, Prose, and Commentaries*, containing forty-seven of Larson's works and eleven of her illustrations. *Days Forgotten* was published in 2006.

Art-Making

Dance

Literary

Media

Music

Performance

Visual

"It was a new and wonderful feeling to have a purpose that went beyond standard coursework and to engage in a project that can change the actual legacy that a person leaves behind," she recalls. "I hope that other senior citizens who discover *Days Forgotten* will be given the hope that their voices can be heard as well."

Melvin Larson reviews a rough draft of his book, *Days Forgotten*. Photo by Chamira Jones

Melvin Larson holds one of the first official copies of *Days Forgotten*.   Photo by Bonnie Larson

Melvin reads aloud from a rough draft of *Days Forgotten*. Photo by Chamira Jones

"There is no question that intellectual fruits... are the most difficult to nurture. It is my hope that I can plant at least one seed which will prosper. This will grow into a tree, which will shade and succor some other human. More significantly, this tree will be the source of shelter and comfort for the whole human race."

– Melvin Larson

Partner Institution

Turner Senior Resource Center houses the community outreach programs of the University of Michigan Geriatrics Center. Staffed with social workers, volunteers, and other professionals who specialize in working with older adults, the Center includes a housing bureau, a learning-in-retirement program, an Asian outreach program, a caregiver resource center, an art gallery, and many other community programs. Melvin Larson was a participant in Coffeehouse, a support and education group for older adults with memory loss.

ARTIST PROFILE

Since graduating magna cum laude from the University of Michigan School of Art and Design, where she won the Martin Luther King Jr. Spirit Award, Chamira Jones has illustrated many books and served as creative coordinator for a major publisher.

Chamira Jones

"From an early age, I knew that art would play a large part in my life, although others often told me that it was not the most lucrative career choice, to say the least. For this reason, I briefly considered engineering and architecture, but at the end of the day I always came back to art. After high school, I rolled up my sleeves and decided to go for a Bachelor of Fine Arts at the University of Michigan School of Art and Design. Four years later, I had earned my degree and was ready to pursue it professionally. Since then, I have never regretted that choice. Not once." – Chamira Jones

Other artwork by Chamira Jones can be seen at www.chamirastudios.com

March 9, 2006: Opening day of the *Days Forgotten* exhibit at the Turner Resource Center in Ann Arbor. A crowd of friends, staff, and University of Michigan students gathered to hear Melvin Larson speak.
Photo by Satoru Takahashi

CONTACT INFORMATION

For information about contacting Chamira Jones, see Appendix A, page 215.

"I have often seen quite demented patients recognize and respond vividly to paintings and delight in the act of painting at a time when they are scarcely responsive, disoriented, and out of it."

– Oliver Sacks

Garrison Institute on Aging, Texas Tech University Health Sciences Center, Lubbock, Texas

BOOM: Housecalls about Medicine and Graying America

Garrison Institute on Aging,
Texas Tech University Health Sciences Center
Lubbock, Texas

A medical student's video documentary about elders increases her peers' awareness and sensitivity.

A still frame of interviewee, Ben, taken from the video by Renée Buchanan

Like citizens of towns and cities everywhere, the elder citizens of Lubbock, Texas have a lot to say about doctors, health, and healthcare. But no one had ever asked them – at least no one with a video camera – until second-year medical student Renée Buchanan came by.

Interviewing seniors in their homes, in assisted living facilities, and in nursing homes, Buchanan recorded many hours of footage which she then edited to a half-hour video program in which her subjects speak in their own distinctive voices about aging, fear, hope, and their strategies for obtaining the best treatment they can.

She first showed her video, *BOOM: Housecalls about Medicine and Graying America*, to a class of 150 second-year medical students at the school she was attending, Texas Tech University Health Sciences Center. It received a standing ovation, and the school's director of interdisciplinary programs on aging says that it increased the interest in geriatric practice and geriatric issues among those students.

One student's comments in an email to Buchanan articulated the film's impact on him, and are representative of many comments she received:

> It was really wonderful to hear thoughts from each of these people about what we can do to facilitate trust in the relationship, aspects of life and death in our practice, and the little things that can make a huge difference – laughter, a touch, talking about their personal history instead of just medical history, and being respectful of their time, too. This is something that every medical student

Art-Making

Dance

Literary

Media

Music

Performance

Visual

should watch – thank you for putting together such a beautiful and thoughtful presentation on behalf of those who have done so much in the time before us to ensure we have such incredible opportunities for the future.

"Practicing medicine is an art as well as a science," Buchanan observes. "I think videos like mine can help students – and practitioners, too – get in touch with the 'art' part in important ways." *BOOM* has been acquired by medical-school libraries and has been previewed by medical educators who are considering starting their own film projects with students.

A still frame of interviewee, Jean, taken from the video by Renée Buchanan

A still frame of interviewees, Gene and Imogene, taken from the video by Renée Buchanan

"As a member of a medical school teaching faculty for many years...I have watched students become increasingly driven to 'pass the test,' which is in our case the USMLE licensing examinations.... [I]n the first several years of medical school, one has to drag them away from the multiple-choice questions. Ms. Buchanan's video did that for my class. It also reminded me that there are students out there who are more concerned with holding a patient's hand than reading their laboratory results."

– Suzanne Graham, M.D., associate professor of pathology

Partner Institution

Texas Tech University Health Sciences Center (TTUHSC) is a five-school university located on four campuses and two academic centers, including schools of medicine, nursing, pharmacy, allied health sciences, and biomedical sciences. The Garrison Institute on Aging is the keystone of a major TTUHSC initiative to help seniors successfully approach and extend the years of quality life; it has divisions focused on research, education, clinical service, and the advancement of quality in long-term care.

Renée Buchanan
Photo by Jason Sifford

ARTIST PROFILE

Before she earned her medical degree, Renée Buchanan received a Master's degree in psychology. In 2008 she began her residency in neurology at the University of Iowa Hospitals and Clinics.

"I need a community that welcomes my creative parts along with my medical parts.... In my futuristic utopia, the movies are part of my medical practice, a testimony to what people overcome, what their struggles are now and what they have been."

"Medical educators could become a lot more creative. Give medical students the chance to choose their art. There is nothing creative about a weekly mandatory humanities lecture. Expose medical students to music therapy and art therapy and child therapy during the medical curriculum. And don't forget to invite the artists!"

CONTACT INFORMATION

For information about contacting Renée Buchanan, see Appendix A, page 215.

"Love and compassion are necessities, not luxuries. Without them, humanity cannot survive."

— The Dalai Lama

A still frame of interviewee, Kay, taken from the video by Renée Buchanan

"We are caught in an inescapable network of mutuality, tied in a single garment of destiny."

— Martin Luther King, Jr.

Projects Serving the Public

8

Projects Serving the Public

An image from *Expanding the Vision through Photography*
Photo by Joey Paynter

By raising awareness about health issues and inspiring healthy behaviours, the powerful communication capabilities of the arts can help citizens make wiser, better-informed choices.

"[I]n the posters and billboards...we see the power of community in the brave images and messages of compassionate citizens. They are the ones who dare to say "We Care" in letters as big as the rainbow. Our power to heal as individuals and as a society is deeply rooted in the power of such compassion."

— Adriana Diaz, artist and board member of *Health Through Art*

"Artistic growth is, more than it is anything else, a refining of the sense of truthfulness. The stupid believe that to be truthful is easy; only the artist, the great artist, knows how difficult it is."

– Willa Cather

"We Care"
Artist: Becky Collins

Health Through Art

Health & Human Resource Education Center, Alameda County
Berkeley, California

"Respect"
Artist: Betty Bishop

A public art program deeply rooted in its community brings health awareness to millions.

When a devastating earthquake struck the San Francisco Bay Area in 1989, Tisha Kenny narrowly avoided being crushed under the collapse of a freeway viaduct that killed 42 people. At home later that night, huddled in a corner of her apartment as aftershocks rumbled through, she found herself saying aloud, "Okay, I get it. There's something I'm supposed to do."

She already had done a lot, as a nurse, a public health administrator, an accomplished ikebana flower arranger, and a painter. But she saw that she could help her city recover from tragedy, fear, and health-related problems through a community-based arts program.

"Health Through Art: Signs of Recovery" was the first manifestation of her understanding. In its current version, *Health Through Art*, focusing on public awareness of health and well-being issues, has overseen the posting of over eight thousand community and transit billboards, organized over fifteen hundred roving art exhibits, distributed over twenty thousand promotional items, and created direct contacts with more than half a million people.

Kenny says, "The project's mission is to be a catalyst for social change through reclaiming the powerful mainstream media for the promotion of healthy choices – free from prejudice, substance abuse, and violence – that celebrate the inherent sacredness of our individual self, family, culture, and community."

Art-Making
Dance
Literary
Media
Music
Performance
Visual

Health Through Art is deeply rooted in Bay Area communities, receiving many hundreds of submissions in response to its every-other-year calls for art and its frequent special solicitations. Themes are selected through extensive community-centered focus groups, and winning entries are chosen by a multi-cultural, multi-ethnic community advisory board. *Health Through Art* has collaborated with over three hundred community organizations, programs, and other projects, and it has sponsored two inner-city murals in Oakland, California.

Tisha Kenny says, "As we have opened ourselves to the needs of the community, we have been gifted with a deluge of gorgeous imagery and messaging relating to all aspects of personal and community health – not only nutrition, substance abuse, and environmental issues, but also violence, racism, bullying, and stereotyping. We have also seen the positive side presented, too, in works promoting self-esteem, respect, mindfulness, and personal responsibility."

Anne Bacon submitted this work to *Health Through Art* in 2002. She served as *Health Through Art's* program coordinator from 2005 to 2008, and is currently a member of its Community Advisory Board.

Anne Bacon with her work, "It Will Rain – BUT – That's What Umbrellas are for"

"Respect, Hope, Love... Everyone Needs Some"
Artist: Annika Nelson

A 92-page book describing the history of *Health Through Art* and including many color images is available at www.healththroughart.org

Partner Institution

The Health & Human Resource Education Center (HHREC), located in Berkeley, California, blends health, art, media, and community residents to create a community-based prevention education strategy that addresses collective physical, mental, and spiritual healing. In addition to Health Through Art, HHREC operates the Black Women's Media Project and has conducted several special mental health and substance abuse prevention projects in conjunction with Alameda County Behavioral Health Care Services.

ARTIST PROFILES

Tisha Kenny
Photo by Anne Bacon

Tisha Kenny co-founded the Health & Human Resource Education Center in 1984 along with Joel Clark and Larry Williams. She developed the *Health Through Art* project in 1989 and has been its executive director since then.

"It is our belief that healing arises out of understanding, and that understanding occurs when a path is cleared for the heart and mind to synchronize their perspectives. We believe that human beings possess the power and creativity to bring about enormous change and have great words of wisdom to speak, if those in positions to amplify their voices are willing to listen. Artwork allows us to step outside the boundaries of right and wrong and to find validation for a perspective that just may save our lives, or the life of someone we hadn't known was listening."

Adriana Diaz, Health Through Art Founding Community Advisory Board Member 1989-2008, and Health Through Art Project Coordinator 2008 to present
Photo by Tisha Kenny

Current Health Through Art program coordinator Adriana Diaz, a founding member of the Community Advisory Board, is an accomplished painter, a college-level educator, a Creative Life Coach, and the author of **Freeing the Creative Spirit, Drawing on the Power of Art to Tap the Magic and Wisdom Within.** She has been a member of the Health Through Art team for 20 years.

CONTACT INFORMATION

For information about contacting Tisha Kenny at *Health Through Art*, see Appendix A, page 215.

"Put simply, *Health Through Art* would be impossible without the dedicated support, brilliant ideas, and exceptional leadership of its Community Advisory Board. The Community Advisory Board is the root structure of HTA. This all-volunteer board works with the project staff as the primary decision-making body of the project. The board works together with a creative heart with a joy of creating support for healthy choices and a positive vision of life in the labyrinth of today's urban environment."

– Tisha Kenny

"Be Yourself, Be Real"
Artist: Laura Wheelock

Projects Serving the Public
Projects Serving the Public
Projects Serving the Public
Projects Serving the Public
Projects Serving the Public
Projects Serving the Public
Projects Serving the Public
Projects Serving the Public

"No form of art goes beyond
ordinary consciousness as
film does, straight to our
emotions, deep into the
twilight room of the soul."

– Ingmar Bergman

Projects Serving the Public
Projects Serving the Public
Projects Serving the Public
Projects Serving the Public
Projects Serving the Public
Projects Serving the Public
Projects Serving the Public

203 Days

Vi and Milton Weinstein Hospice
Atlanta, Georgia

Sarah Neider and Kaye Green
Photo by Bailey Barash

An unflinching video documentary promotes awareness of hospice and end-of-life issues.

When Bailey Barash and Sarah Neider first met, Neider, 89 years old, was living at her daughter's home with a terminal heart condition. Doctors said she had six months to live. She was cared for by her daughter, Kaye Green, and by staff from the Vi and Milton Weinstein Hospice, in Atlanta.

Barash was a volunteer at the Weinstein hospice, honoring a commitment she had made after caring for her father and mother as cancer took his life and emphysema and asthma claimed hers. She had also worked full time as Executive Producer of Science News at CNN.

Barash filmed the last days of Neider's life for her documentary, *203 Days*. Neider's decline and death are unflinchingly portrayed, along with the unstinting love and care provided by her daughter and the sustaining attention provided by other family members and hospice staff.

Called "a brave, intimate, and tender film that shows both the poignancy and the difficulties of a person's last year," *203 Days* has been used in many settings to increase awareness and sensitivity regarding hospice care and the last days of life. As increasing numbers of persons become candidates for hospice care, the film provides an exemplary service in alerting the public to the importance of end-of-life care and the difficulties faced by family caregivers.

In 2007, the film won the prestigious CINE Golden Eagle Award, and it also was made available for viewing, accompanied by a study guide, at the internet website of the Univer-

Art-Making

Dance

Literary

Media

Music

Performance

Visual

sity of Connecticut Health Center.[1] Joseph M. Civetta, M.D., Professor of Surgery at the University of Connecticut School of Medicine, said,

"*203 Days* is very powerful, especially for young students in all aspects of caring professions. They do not have any experience with dying, either the human dynamics or the physiology. The film will get them thinking – and it will be good for them."

A screening of the film, followed by discussion, was evaluated by those who attended. 98 percent of the respondents said it would assist them in discussing end-of-life issues with loved ones, that it gave them a better understanding of hospice services, and that they would consider using hospice to care for a loved one.

Elizabeth, Kaye, and Joanna (left to right) help
Sarah light the Chanukah candles.
Photo by Bailey Barash

Sarah and her son Jerry and daughter Kaye
light Shabbos candles.
Photo by Bailey Barash

Sarah and her granddaughters
Photo by Ronald Green

A recent study at Johns Hopkins University showed that a personal caregiver at the end of life spends more than forty-three hours a week helping the loved one and rarely asks for community-based help.

Partner Institution

Since 1999, the Vi and Milton Weinstein Hospice in Atlanta has served almost 500 families with individualized homecare. Talya Bloom, Director of Hospice Services, worked closely with Bailey Barash as Barash created *203 Days*. The Weinstein Hospice is affiliated with the William Bremen Jewish Home, a beneficiary agency of the Jewish Federation of Greater Atlanta. Sarah Neider spent her last days there.

ARTIST PROFILE

Bailey Barash
Photo by Lisa Saul

After 19 years at CNN, Bailey Barash formed her own production company in 1999. Winner of a 2005 CINE Golden Eagle for her independent documentary, *Fried Chicken and Sweet Potato Pie*, she has studied and taught journalism in Hawaii, the Czech Republic, Slovakia, Romania, and Hungary. Her most recent production is the feature-length documentary, *The AIDS Chronicles – Here to Represent*, which focuses on the social and cultural impact of HIV/AIDS on the African-American community of Atlanta. About *203 Days*, she says:

There are a lot of things that people don't want to think about but will be forced to think about, especially if they have older parents who are getting on and may be frail. It's very painful to have to think about these things, and within families there are always conflicts; a lot of these conflicts can be ignored until there's a crisis, but then they have to be dealt with, because they involve the people who are involved in the crisis. I'm very glad that this film is being used in medical schools, in hospices, and other places where there is often too little awareness of the deep human issues that arise at the end of life.

203 Days can be purchased on DVD or VHS tape at www.bbarash.com/bb_203days.htm.

"Thank you for a meaningful and powerful presentation. Your work is appreciated more than you will ever know."

– Family member of a hospice patient

Sarah Neider with her daughter, Kaye
Photo by David Neider

CONTACT INFORMATION

For information about contacting Bailey Barash, see Appendix A, page 215.

1. The website is http://fitsweb.uchc.edu/days/days.html

"The primary benefit of practicing any art, whether well or badly, is that it enables one's soul to grow."

– Kurt Vonnegut

Mural Drawing at a Medical School

Royal Free and University College Medical School
London, England

Mural detail, left corner
Photo by Rosanna Wellesley

A medical student's artwork enlivens the human body for her peers.

After attending Magdalen College in Oxford for her pre-clinical medical studies, Rosanna Wellesley undertook a bachelor of fine arts degree at the prestigious Ruskin School of Drawing and Fine Art. She then returned to medical school at University College London to complete her training as a doctor.

From her dual perspective as an artist and a medical student, Wellesley perceived that she and her fellow students were learning about the human body as an objective, mechanical entity, but losing sight of its wonder and mystery. "The job of the doctor is often to divine the invisible," she says, "yet despite this necessity for a certain type of imagination there is little capacity for a more playful imaginative attitude toward what we are learning."

With encouragement from school authorities, she began drawing a large indoor mural in a central area of her medical school, at the site of an old elevator shaft. The mural was roughly thirty feet wide and ten feet high, depicting the body in a variety of forms: "tumbling bodies, spiraling out as they are dissected away," as she describes it. Over the course of the two weeks that she worked on the mural, many students stopped to discuss it with her, and she revised her original design in response to their observations and suggestions.

In a survey Wellesley later conducted among first-year medical students, 41 percent of the respondents reported that the drawing had contributed to their understanding of the human body, and one in five respondents said the mural caused

Art-Making
Dance
Literary
Media
Music
Performance
Visual

them to consider patients' bodies differently. 88 percent said that art has a place in the experience of healthcare.

83 percent of the students said they had stopped by to watch as Wellesley created the mural. "The most important outcomes of the project were the informal discussions that took place as the drawing was done," she says. "Medical students do an awful lot of book learning for anatomy and we've lost that more playful, empathetic, and imaginative attitude toward the subject. With the mural, they hopefully get to see something which helps them explore the things they are learning through books in a more creative way."

Although it was intended that Rosanna Wellesley's mural would be painted over as part of a renovation project, it has remained in place outside the medical school's library.
Photo by Rosanna Wellesley

Mural, left wall, view from corridor
Photo by Rosanna Wellesley

"Important to the medical students' experience of the drawing was also that the mural was to be destroyed a few months after completion. This served to shift the focus of attention from the drawing itself to the process of its creation."

– Rosanna Wellesley

Partner Institution

The Royal Free and University College Medical School, in London, was created by the 1998 merger of two separate medical schools. It has three London campuses and a new sixteen-story hospital, which opened in 2005.

ARTIST PROFILE

Rosanna Wellesley graduated as a doctor in 2004 and has been working in hospitals since. In 2008 Wellesley spent ten months in Zambia working as a medical registrar in the University Teaching Hospital, and lecturing for the medical school there. She is currently working as a doctor in Tower Hamlets, the most deprived borough of London, and draws regularly in and around the city.

> "Visual art as a participative activity has a massive potential to engage people and develop opinions that passive pieces hung on walls may never achieve outside a gallery setting."

"What makes an arresting anatomical drawing is not just a knowledge of the muscular points of origin and insertion but an emotional awareness of the makeup of the body, how it sweats and breathes and what that means to us. Our own attitudes toward our bodies are dependent on the functioning of them. When we are lucky and healthy, we think nothing of our lungs or our livers or even our feet. Stand on a nail, however, and suddenly the pain forces us to devote an attention to that foot that we had had the luxury of thinking nothing of moments before. So our perspective and understanding of our body is constantly shifting, an intensely subjective experience that varies from moment to moment. I think most people understand this better than doctors." – Rosanna Wellesley

Rosanna Wellesley

"Art is an experience, not an object."

– Robert Motherwell

Mural, back wall detail
Photo by Rosanna Wellesley

CONTACT INFORMATION

For information about contacting Rosanna Wellesley, see Appendix A, page 215.

"All art that really draws us to look at it deeply is spiritual."

– Wendy Beckett

Healthcare Area of Focus:
Neonatal Intensive Care Unit
Photographer: Earl McKinney

Expanding the Vision through Photography

St. Charles Bend Medical Center
Bend, Oregon

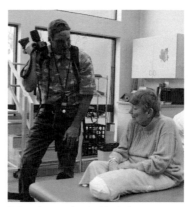

Project photographer Patrick Windsor,
Rehabilitation, with a patient
Photo by Robert Agli

**Photographers'
perspectives demystify
the hospital experience.**

Expanding the Vision
THROUGH PHOTOGRAPHY

Twelve local photographers, given unlimited access, were challenged to find and document the heart of the hospital at St. Charles Medical Center in Bend, Oregon. St. Charles is operated by Cascade Healthcare Community.

Each photographer focused on one functional area within the hospital, seeking a single image that would capture the essence of the service provided there. "The overarching purpose of the project," says St. Charles's Arts in the Hospital coordinator Marlene Alexander, "was to foster discussion of the role of healthcare in our community and our lives, and to demystify the hospital experience so patients and family could approach it realistically, without undue fear or alarm."

The resulting photographs and the overall theme, "Expanding the Vision," were integrated into many aspects of the hospital's operations. Community meetings were held at which the photographs served as a catalyst for discussion. The photographers attended exhibits of their work and other functions to talk about what they had seen and experienced.

The photographs were employed in support of the hospital's capital campaign, "Expanding the Vision: Building for a Healthy Central Oregon," and used at its website and in many of its print publications. During and after the period when the photography was taking place, hospital employees were asked to submit their own written "snapshot observations of positive things." Many of these personal observations were subsequently published in the employee newsletter.

Art-Making

Dance

Literary

Media

Music

Performance

Visual

"Additionally," Marlene Alexander says, "the project provided caregivers with public recognition of the importance of their daily work, and has allowed them to learn more about other areas and services that the hospital provides. This recognition has resulted in a renewed sense of purpose and pride among caregivers at all levels in the organization."

Along with written reflections from the photographers, the images were incorporated into a traveling exhibit that appeared in many Oregon locations over several months. Prints of the photographs were offered for sale, with 30 percent of the proceeds going to the hospital. The project was extensively covered in local and regional publications: *Cascade Arts & Entertainment,* for example, devoted two pages to each photographer's work in twelve consecutive issues.

Bridget McGinn, a member of the St. Charles marketing team and representative to the St. Charles Foundation, coordinated the project as well as playing a major role in its conception. McGinn's work has appeared in national juried shows. Showing her own considerable skills as a photographer, she brought an acute visual perspective to the project team.

Healthcare Area of Focus: Heart and Research
Photographer: Kevin Kubota

Healthcare Area of Focus: Family Birthing Centers
Photographer: Benjamin Edwards, Pixelworks Studios Inc.

"I don't believe I'd be over-romanticizing this project by predicting that individuals who view the final exhibit, with all 12 talented photographers' work, might feel a bit easier the next time they visit St. Charles for any reason.

Comfort comes with contact."

—Benjamin Edwards, Photographer, Pixelworks Studios Inc.
Healthcare Area of Focus: Family Birthing Centers

Partner Institution

St. Charles Bend Medical Center is one of four hospitals in the Cascade Health Community system, which serves more than 240,000 people in a 32,000 square-mile area.

ARTIST PROFILE

Marlene Alexander

Marlene Alexander initiated the first art program at St. Charles Medical Center in 1990, and today she heads its Arts in the Hospital program. She also owns and operates a creative arts school for children.

> "This project was particularly important because it reached people who are 'right-brained' and therefore communicate better with visuals. As part of a capital campaign, the photographs helped us reach a larger population."

Marlene Alexander is also an award-winning painter. Her works can be seen at www.atticgallery.com.

"As the photographers have immersed themselves in their focus areas, preconceived notions have been replaced by the reality of the work that takes place there every day. It is often heartbreaking, painful, and difficult to absorb; and conversely there are times of pure joy and happiness." – Marlene Alexander

"The project offered support and reassurance to ourselves as caregivers during a stressful period [of facing technological, organizational, and community issues], while at the same time reassuring our community and reinforcing our commitment to our mission, transcending financial concerns, union issues, and community politics."

– Eric Alexander, Senior Vice President for Regional Operations and Executive Director, St. Charles Foundation

Healthcare Area of Focus: Emergency Department
Photographer: Hadley McCann

CONTACT INFORMATION

For information about contacting Marlene Alexander, see Appendix A, page 215.

9 Healing from Tragedy

Prayer Flags for Sophia. A neighbor visits Sophia and makes a flag.
Photo by Kate Robertson.

The restorative powers of art can provide solace and
inspiration at times of tragedy. The examples in this
chapter range from a large-scale response by artists to a
natural disaster, to work with the direct and indirect victims
of domestic violence, to helping parents and others cope
with the grief brought on by the death of a child.

"In order to understand how healing happens in the
twenty-first century, we shall look not only at our atoms
and molecules but at consciousness as well. In so
doing, we shall reinvent medicine, adding an ancient
wisdom to modern science." – Larry Dossey, M.D.

"Art washes away from
the soul the dust of
everyday life."

– Pablo Picasso

Halloween masks
Photo by Judy Ginsburgh

Beyond Katrina: Arts in the Shelters

The American Red Cross

"Flood," a piece of art created in the shelters
Photo by Judy Ginsburgh

Arts programs bring solace and healing to thousands of evacuees.

When Hurricane Katrina hit America's gulf coast in 2005, over fifteen thousand evacuees fled to shelters and other housing in Alexandria, Louisiana.

Alexandria resident Judy Ginsburgh, executive director of Alexandria-based Central Louisiana Arts & Healthcare, responded with what she knew best:

> We could bring the same techniques and arts experiences into the shelters that we implement in hospitals. Our goal was to use the arts to help people get beyond their confusion, anger, and fear to move to an emotional place where they could find hope and begin to rebuild their lives.

Ginsburgh put out a call to local artists and contacted Jill Sonke-Henderson, Assistant Director and Artist-in-Residence at the Arts in Medicine program at University of Florida Shands Medical Center. Within a few days she, Sonke-Henderson, and some colleagues trained over seventy artists – some of them evacuees themselves – to begin working with people in the shelters.

First, they helped the evacuees start creating a journey wall mural. For those murals, which became the centerpieces of the healing art at each shelter, individuals created drawings and compositions reflecting their lives and their hopes. Before long, the evacuees were creating origami compositions, making paper-bead jewelry, singing, learning to play musical instruments, doing yoga, journaling, listening to humorous stories, telling their own jokes, and engaging in the full panoply of arts interventions.

Art-Making
Dance
Literary
Media
Music
Performance
Visual

> **"We needed supplies and we needed lots of them. Over the course of two months, we received over $40,000 in donated cash and arts materials."**
>
> – Judy Ginsburgh

Teaching guitar in the Riverfront Center shelter, Alexandria, Louisiana
Photo by Barry Owen

As the evacuees left the shelters, memory of the projects remained with them. Artists visited temporary trailer communities throughout Louisiana, a traveling exhibit of art and poetry from the shelters was created and a book of poetry, quotes, and images titled *Beyond Katrina* has been published. Ginsburgh writes, "Many of our artists have continued their Red Cross training so we are ready at a moment's notice to be a vital part of a first response disaster team."

Journeying wall at the Riverfront Center Shelter
Photo by Judy Ginsburgh

The book, *Beyond Katrina*, is available for purchase. Judy Ginsburgh and others have also created a manual for use in disaster relief efforts, and they are developing a database of artists in disaster-prone areas who could be available in an emergency situation. To learn more, contact her at judy@artsandhealthcare.org

Partner Institution

American Red Cross volunteers cooperated with the artists in many ways. Ginsburgh writes, "The shelters were run by Red Cross volunteers from all over the United States. They were wonderful to work with and we were all amazed with their professionalism, flexibility, and compassion."

Advice and energetic assistance were provided by Jill Sonke-Henderson and others from the exemplary Arts in Medicine program at the University of Florida Shands Medical Center.

ARTIST PROFILE

Judy Ginsburgh

Judy Ginsburgh is the founder and executive director of Central Louisiana Arts & Healthcare, in Alexandria, Louisiana, which provides arts programming at Rapides Regional Medical Center and CHRISTUS St. Frances Cabrini Hospital in Alexandria, Louisiana. Art programming is also provided to an Alexandria-area orthopedic clinic and adult day care center.

Trained in vocal performance at the Indiana University School of Music, she wrote this in 2006:

"Five years ago, I never dreamed that I would be working in the field of arts and healthcare – five years ago, I had never even heard of arts and healthcare. As I look back, there were many instances where I had instinctively used the arts to heal without even knowing it. One situation occurred when my own son was brought to the emergency room with a broken arm. While they were preparing him for surgery, a busload of preschool children arrived at the ER. Their bus had been hit, and although none of the children were seriously injured they all had to be checked out. There was fear and chaos in the waiting room. I sat down in the middle of the children and began singing songs with them. Their tears stopped and they began to have fun. The singing made them less anxious and less afraid. And it also helped me to worry less about my own son."

"I still perform regularly in healthcare settings, particularly in palliative care, and still seeing miracles occur regularly through the power of music."

CONTACT INFORMATION

For information about contacting Judy Ginsburgh at Central Louisiana Arts & Healthcare, see Appendix A, page 215.

"Art condenses the experience we all have as human beings, and, by forming it, makes it significant. We all have an in-built need for harmony and the structures that create harmony. Basically, art is an affirmation of life."

– Trevor Bell

Music man in the Coliseum shelter, Alexandria, Louisiana
Photo by Judy Ginsburgh

"I try to apply colors like words that shape poems, like notes that shape music."

– Joan Miro

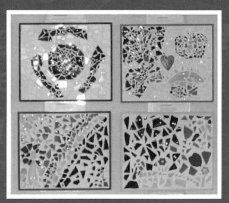

Close up of the mosaic display in the counseling center at the Julian Center. Artists include a variety of groups including a women's therapy group, area churches, student groups, local businesses, and physician groups.

The Domestic Violence Awareness Mosaic Project

The Julian Center
Indianapolis, Indiana

Workshop participants create mosaics for awareness, hope, and healing.

"Moving On" This mosaic shows a turtle making its way... toward the sun. Her shell is strong and protective, and her movement forward to the brightness of a new life is gradual. It is a metaphor for the healing journey taken by victims of domestic violence. *Photo by Karen Gehrman*

The Julian Center

How do you provoke an intellectual and visceral awareness of the tragedy of domestic violence, and a sense of hope in its aftermath? Among groups as diverse as business executives, kindergarten teachers, law-enforcement personnel, family-practice doctors, civic groups, and middle-school students, Liza Hyatt and Christine Arthur accomplished that awareness through the *Domestic Violence Awareness Mosaic Project*.

Using pieces of shattered household china under the theme "Putting the Pieces Back Together," participants in workshops led by Hyatt and Arthur created mosaics depicting the possibilities of healing after domestic violence. "Frequently, adult women survivors of childhood sexual abuse, domestic violence, and sexual assault describe themselves as shattered, broken," Hyatt explains. "They also describe their anger in terms of wanting to break things, or actually choosing to break things. Bits-and-pieces mosaic is superb way to capture those feelings and imagine positive possibilities."

More than seventy mosaics created by the various groups were incorporated into a traveling exhibit shown in community centers, libraries, art centers, professional conferences, and other venues. The project, originally conceived as lasting one year, went on for six years as more and more groups requested opportunities to participate and learn from it.

Art-Making
Dance
Literary
Media
Music
Performance
Visual

Many of the completed mosaics now hang in the corridors and offices of the Indianapolis-based sponsoring organization, The Julian Center, a nonprofit agency that provides counseling, safe shelter, and education for women and children who are survivors of domestic violence and abuse.

"A group of six kids living in the transitional housing program of The Julian Center's shelter worked to create a mosaic with an image of a house containing a family inside looking out through the windows. They described the family as having learned new ways to get along; the dad found other ways of expressing his feelings without hurting family members.... Making the mosaic helped them to feel hopeful that good changes could happen in their lives/families in the future."

– Christine Arthur

Mosaic display in the hallway connecting The Julian Center Administration with Indianapolis Metropolitan Police Department's Domestic Violence Task Force. Artists include therapists, youth in juvenile detention, middle-school students, church members, and survivors of domestic violence.

"Untouchable" by middle-school students. This mosaic shows two sides of a face. One, the false side which victims must show to the world, while hidden inside them rests the other, the ugliness of fear and despair. It shows that each individual must find the courage to transform their situation and to restore their inner beauty and self-respect.

Partner Institution

Since 1975, The Julian Center in Indianapolis, Indiana has served women and children victims of abuse and assault. It offers counseling, a 24-hour shelter, and other services.

ARTIST PROFILES

Christine Arthur is a facilitator of the Mosaic Project at The Julian Center. She has practiced both verbal and art psychotherapy since 1996, and specializes in the treatment of women and children who have experienced trauma. She has incorporated mosaic-making into both individual therapy and open art studio formats.

An art therapist, poet, and professional storyteller since 1989, Liza Hyatt began making mosaics in 1997. She has her own arts-based private practice today, specializing in community mosaics but also providing storytelling and art therapy. She currently leads workshops for schoolchildren, congregations, and faith groups, and for cancer patients at the Indiana University Melvin and Bren Simon Cancer Center.

"Mosaics immediately capture the attention of all who see them. They interest us because we all know what it is like to be broken in some way. But mosaics also show us that from brokenness itself beauty is made. In other words, we have to be broken open in order to become more whole." – Liza Hyatt

Christine Arthur and Liza Hyatt

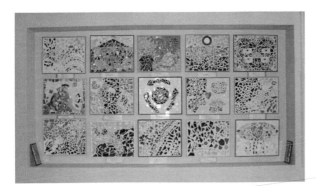

Mosaic display in the counseling center at The Julian Center. Artists include a variety of groups including a women's therapy group, area churches, student groups, local businesses, and physician groups.

Liza Hyatt on a retreat for hematology/oncology nurses, doctors, and treatment team members at Indiana University Simon Cancer Center in which she facilitated mosaic-making to help them explore "true collaboration" as a team.
Photo by Gary Schmitt

CONTACT INFORMATION

For information about contacting Christine Arthur or Liza Hyatt, see Appendix A, page 215.

"Our sorrows and wounds are healed only when we touch them with compassion."

– Buddha

Flag-making
Photo by Kate Robertson

Prayer Flags for Sophia

Pathways Hospice
Sunnyvale, California

Handmade prayer flags express a community's love, caring, support, and remembrance for a stricken child and her family.

Prayer flags surround the family with beauty
Photo by Kate Robertson

Sophia's Garden
HEALING IN COMMUNITY

In February of 2003 Karen Herzog and Richard Sachs brought their twenty-month-old daughter, Sophia, home for hospice care. Sophia suffered from Neimann-Pick Type A, an incurable disorder that cuts infants' life spans to two or three years.

Home-care nurse Deborah Quevedo describes more of this story, from her perspective:

> I could see that Sophia's illness was deeply affecting her parents and family. Not only were they exhausted from caring for her around the clock, but they were scared that she might stop breathing at any moment. A big part of my job was to monitor her breathing.
>
> I instantly fell in love with Sophia. Her loveliness was juxtaposed with a yellow feeding tube and her helplessness: she couldn't lift or turn her head. It was heartbreaking to see the disparity of innocent preciousness with serious disease. I wondered if I would be able to emotionally handle caring for her.
>
> Immediately, I found that caring for Sophia was unlike anything I had ever experienced in my 25-year nursing career. Sophia and her family were surrounded by a loving and supportive community. People came to their home every day to make prayer flags and bring food.
>
> This support went on for many months until there were 150 flags hanging in the house. In spite of the tragedy, a very hopeful milieu was created.... Her home was transformed into a sacred space.

The idea for the prayer flags came from Robin Modlin, an artist who is also a chaplain. Sophia's mother Karen Herzog tells that part of the story:

Art-Making
Dance
Literary
Media
Music
Performance
Visual

Sophia with her father, Richard Sachs
Photo by Kate Robertson

After another sleepless night with Sophia, Robin had an idea for a ritual that would embrace the community that was pouring into our home to give creative expression of the pain and love for Sophia and our family. That same afternoon, Robin arrived with colorful squares of cotton cloth and a wide assortment of art and craft supplies. She gently and skillfully led the house full of family and friends through a celebratory ceremony to capture the spirit of Sophia and the meaning of her life. Then hands, scissors, feathers, beads, glue, pipe cleaners, patterned fabric, and a rainbow of fabric paint went flying around the living and dining rooms.

Strangers started talking, crying, singing, and collaborating in unison. Friends with fallen bridges mended fences. Frightened faces, like mine, softened to a solemn, peaceful glow.

The creative community outpouring manifested in the prayer flags that afternoon has grown since then…. Blessings for Sophia reach beyond geographical and physical boundaries. Like pollen in the wind, they propagate the essence of the human spirit: the quest for meaning and healing.

Sophia passed away in 2005. Prayer flags in her honor were created and displayed throughout the world – in Bulgaria, Tibet, Switzerland, Fiji, Japan, China, and Australia. In Kuwait, a prayer flag was flown at the first children's hospice and palliative care center in the Arab world.

Sophia's father, Richard Sachs, observes, "Instead of Sophia being the focus of our community's fear and helplessness, she became a wellspring of creativity. The flags flying in and around our house embody the compassion and faith of our community as a whole. Each of the flags creates a lovely note – the tone created by the essential human spirit of the child in every one of us."

"The project was a double gift," says Dr. Barbara Sourkes, director of the pediatric palliative care program at Lucile Packard Children's Hospital at Stanford. "Each individual had the sense of 'giving' to Sophia and her family, and the creative self-expression was an outlet for each person's complex feelings. It is in this sense that the Prayer Flag project is most profoundly a healing project: each creation is a gift that allowed the individual to create wishes for Sophia and her family, and – as the project developed – to witness the growth of a community. For me, this is the essence of the healing arts."

Partner Institution

Pathways Hospice, based in Sunnyvale, California, offered one of the first hospice programs in the United States. Today it delivers care services throughout the San Francisco Bay Area.

Robin Modlin

ARTIST PROFILE

While Robin Modlin was working as a chaplain at Stanford's Lucile Packard Children's Hospital, three pediatric liver transplant patients died during one week. Modlin – who herself has a child with a life-threatening disease, cystic fibrosis – initiated a prayer flag project to deal with the grief and loss that so many were experiencing. "The result," she writes, "was a magical display that flew on the roof garden of the hospital for a month. It truly was inspiring and uplifting for all involved."

Today she is working independently, creating her own artworks as well as designing participatory healing arts projects with Sophia's Garden Foundation. The flags project has grown within the Foundation into StoryFlags, an international online and offline community-building project (www.StoryFlags.com).

"The use of prayer flags is a traditional practice of Tibetan Buddhism. Throughout the Himalayas colorful flags hang in the countryside. Prayers for peace, compassion, and healing are printed on the flags with the understanding that as they fly the wind carries their beautiful messages out to the world."

– Robin Modlin

Prayer flags fly at Lucile Packard Children's Hospital.

A CD of music based on the genetic code for Sophia's DNA was created by Herb Moore. Titled *"Sophia's Garden,"* it is available for purchase. Moore writes, "In spite of incredible life challenges, Sophia brought an abundance of joy and wisdom to so many who entered her 'garden.'"

An example of a "Courage Doll"

In one recent project, Robin Modlin and eight other mothers of children with cystic fibrosis worked together over nine months to create "Courage Dolls."

In the first month, each artist created a doll's head, which was then passed to another artist who created the doll's body during the second month. At the end of nine months, each artist had created a part of each completed doll.

CONTACT INFORMATION

For information about contacting Robin Modlin, see Appendix A, page 215

"Using creativity when dealing with disease can help to unlock hidden emotions and provide a safe way to share one's concerns. It gives a sense of doing something in situations where many times one feels helpless. You do not need to be a great artist to create a prayer flag or a courage doll. It only requires opening your heart and the willingness to share your love and care." – Robin Modlin

A nonprofit organization begun in Sophia's honor – Sophia's Garden Foundation – offers online advice and innovative tools to families of children diagnosed with life-threatening illnesses at www.sophiasgarden.org.

Dianne brings Sophia's flag to Sophia, Bulgaria
Photo by Richard B. Moss, M.D.

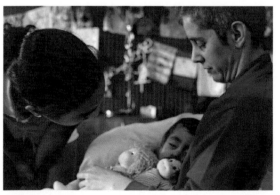

Sophia with her mother, Karen, and her cousin Leilani
Photo by Kate Robertson

Healing from Tragedy
Healing from Tragedy
Healing from Tragedy
Healing from Tragedy
Healing from Tragedy
Healing from Tragedy
Healing from Tragedy
Healing from Tragedy
Healing from Tragedy
Healing from Tragedy
Healing from Tragedy
Healing from Tragedy
Healing from Tragedy
Healing from Tragedy
Healing from Tragedy
Healing from Tragedy
Healing from Tragedy

"When we give
ourselves over
completely to the
spirit of the dance,
it becomes
a prayer."

– Gabrielle Roth

Healing from Tragedy Healing from Tragedy Healing from Tragedy Healing from Tragedy Healing from Tragedy Healing from Tragedy Healing from Tragedy Healing from Tragedy Healing from Tragedy Healing from Tragedy Healing from Tragedy Healing from Tragedy Healing from Tragedy Healing from Tragedy Healing from Tragedy Healing from Tragedy Healing from Tragedy Healing from Tragedy Healing from Tragedy

"Photography takes an instant out of time, altering life by holding it still."

– Dorothea Lange

Photographer Jeff Dykehouse
develops an image.

Emily's Big Picture Project

Hospice of Michigan
Grand Rapids, Michigan

A family portrait
Photo by Jeff Dykehouse

A photographer creates free portraits for families with terminally-ill children.

Emily was just fourteen months old when she passed. She had battled leukemia her entire life. Within hours of her passing it became clear that we didn't have enough pictures of our little sweetie. We had some but just not enough; not many that really captured the real Emily. We didn't have a nice family portrait either. We were too busy taking care of her I guess, it just wasn't something we thought about, her being gone. I wish someone would have told us that we should be taking more pictures and that we should have a family portrait taken, because before we knew it, it was too late.

Jeff Dykehouse determined that what he learned too late after his daughter's death would not afflict other parents of dying children. He left his job as an academic administrator and turned his lifelong interest in photography into Emily's Big Picture Project, creating free portraits of young hospice patients with their families. Since 2006 he and other volunteer photographers have provided over 150 mounted, matted, and framed 16" x 20" family photographs to young children and their families.

The project has expanded to include adult hospice patients who are parents of young children. The project began in conjunction with the state's largest hospice provider, Hospice of Michigan. Its ambitious goal is to make sure every pediatric hospice family in Michigan has the opportunity to have a portrait done, and that every adult hospice patient in Michigan who has young children has the opportunity to have a family portrait.

Art-Making
Dance
Literary
Media
Music
Performance
Visual

Collection of photographs from *Emily's Big Picture Project*

Dykehouse's images from the project have been exhibited in over a dozen cities. His image, *Dustin Being Brave,* won first place in the National Association of Children's Hospitals photo contest.

"Dustin Being Brave"
Photo by Jeff Dykehouse

Gallery features photographs from *Emily's Big Picture Project,* highlighting the award-winning image, "Dustin Being Brave"

Partner Institution

Hospice of Michigan serves terminally-ill individuals in 45 counties throughout the state. Headquartered in Detroit, it is the largest hospice in Michigan and the second-largest nonprofit hospice in the country.

ARTIST PROFILE

Jeff Dykehouse owns Dykehouse Photography in Grand Rapids, Michigan.

"By the grace of God I've managed to capture at least one image at each photo session that captures the personality and peacefulness of each child. The parents tell me they can see their child's spirit in their eyes. These portraits are to help the parents and the entire family heal." – Jeff Dykehouse

Jeff Dykehouse

"From the very beginning, I made a pledge not to accept any money from the families I work with. Many of the families I work with are poor, some do however have the financial means but I feel very strongly that these families should not be burdened with having to even discuss any payment for what is being done. It is a gift and anyone dealing with these families will have to make the same pledge – to never accept any money from families."

"I sometimes get cards from families after their child has passed. These cards bring tears to my eyes just thinking about them. The families tell me how much their portrait means to them, how it helped them get through very difficult times, how it helped them heal! Wow! How fortunate I am to be able to help these families! It's very clear to me that this is the type of work I was put on earth to do. This is my life's work and I can't imagine doing anything else."

CONTACT INFORMATION

For information about contacting Jeff Dykehouse at Emily's Big Picture Project, see Appendix A, page 215.

Mother and daughter
Photo by Jeff Dykehouse

Family portrait
Photo by Jeff Dykehouse

Part III

Making it Happen

"My life belongs to the whole community, and as long as I live it is my privilege to do for it whatever I can."

– George Bernard Shaw

Art project from *Art While You Wait*

"High-impact arts programs do not just happen. They require collaboration between the artist and the organization, designed to achieve agreed-upon objectives."

– page 202

A Roadmap to Create Effective and Sustainable Arts Programs

Nine key steps are essential for building strong and enduring arts programs.

Exempla Good Samaritan Medical Center, Lafayette, Colorado
Artist: Carol Schneider Fennel

As the preceding case examples show, high-impact arts projects are very diverse in the type of art intervention used, the healthcare organization or patient group involved, and the objectives achieved. Many of the projects described evolved from the commitment and creativity of an individual artist who desired to meet a specific healthcare need. However successful they were, we believe there are some key steps that an organization should take to develop and sustain an effective arts program that has the capacity to measurably improve the care or the care experience of patients and the people who care for them. In so doing, an effective arts program can add value to the overall healthcare organization.

This chapter presents a nine-step roadmap for an organization to build strong, effective, sustainable arts programs. Where possible, artists should be active participants.

Step 1. Create a multidisciplinary team to lead the design of the program.

An engaged and committed team greatly increases the likelihood of achieving maximum impact from an arts program. When forming such a team, we believe the key success ingredients are as follows:

Top-leadership involvement. Ideally, the team will be chaired by a senior executive with a strong interest in arts programs. A representative of the organization's charitable foundation should be involved, since the long-term success and expansion of arts programs usually requires fundraising.

Broad representation. Diverse representation of internal and external stakeholders is vital. Internally, we recommend a physician, a nurse, a foundation representative, an administrative executive, and representatives from such functions as chaplaincy, patient services, marketing or public relations, and facilities.

Externally, we recommend members of community arts agencies (city, county, and sometimes state), representatives of local museums, and heads of arts departments of local colleges or universities. Prominent public-spirited citizens and potential donors also make excellent team members. Up to 24 members might participate on a well-run team if an effective committee structure is used.

Champions. Staff and community members who are passionate, articulate advocates of arts programs can contribute greatly to the program's effectiveness.

Access to other decision-making bodies. The team must be able to present its recommendations to other individuals or teams whose work will be affected – for example, to clinical teams, quality and safety personnel, facilities and planning, or key executives.

Patient and family advisory groups. In some organizations where patient and family advisory groups are in place, the arts projects should be reviewed by that group as well, to ensure that the project is being designed from the patient's perspective.

Experienced guidance. Some institutions are blessed with experienced leaders who have designed and implemented successful arts programs. For organizations that do not possess such experience, hiring a professional healthcare arts consultant to lead or facilitate the process is valuable. Effective consultants lead, guide, and advise, but they do not sell art or make final decisions.

Step 2. Develop a mission statement and strategic goals.

Similar to any substantial organizational undertaking, decisions about arts programs should be guided by an agreed-upon mission and strategic goals that are congruent with the overall mission and strategies of the organization. Mission statements describe the overall intent of the arts program. Here are some examples of mission statements adopted by major healthcare organizations for their arts programs:

> "To create an environment where the arts coexist with people, processes, and with purpose...to create an experience with such compelling value that this hospital is the provider of choice for staff, patients, physicians, and employers."

> "This hospital will use the arts to create an environment supportive of health and healing for patients, staff, and visitors."

The program's *strategic goals* should enumerate the practical outcomes toward which the program is directed. They should support identified priorities of the organization. Examples might include:

- Improve patient satisfaction
- Improve family and visitor satisfaction
- Improve staff satisfaction

Kaiser Permanente, La Mesa, California
Artist: Mary Lynn Dominguez

- Reduce perception of waiting time
- Reduce perception of pain and anxiety
- Reduce need for pain medication
- Reduce need for anesthesia
- Support the healing process
- Improve communication between patients and staff
- Strengthen the organization's brand in the marketplace
- Increase community engagement and support
- Reinforce institutional values or faith-based mission
- Attract new donors of all economic and social backgrounds

The mission statement and strategic goals should speak directly to the organization's hopes and aspirations. They provide a reference point for decisions about what projects to initiate, fund, and implement.

Step 3. Select the arts project(s) and determine expected outcomes.

Scripps Mercy Hospital,
Chula Vista, California
Artist: Li Tie

From a review of the literature, websites, solicitation of ideas from artists, and other sources, a project or projects should be identified to meet stated goals. To begin, select a project with a high likelihood of success. There should be clear evidence that the selected project or projects will cost-effectively accomplish the desired ends. A growing body of research is available through the Center for Health Design[1] and the Society for the Arts in Healthcare.[2]

Explicit outcome measures should be established, based on those used to assess similar existing programs. A variety of quantitative and qualitative evaluation methods should be considered. It is advisable to collaborate with the organization's research department or an academic partner to develop appropriate protocols. For some ideas about possible ways to assess project outcomes, see the sidebar "Some Ways of Measuring Project Outcomes" on page 199.

Once a project has been approved and outcome measures selected, baseline data should be collected to provide for future comparisons. Evaluation must take place within the existing organizational structures. For example, if clinical indicators such as blood pressure, heart rate and/or blood cortisol levels are to be measured, approval from the organization's

Scripps Mercy Hospital, Chula Vista, California
Artist: Karen Heyl

Institutional Review Board will likely be needed. In that case, a principal investigator will have to be appointed to lead the project. The IRB requirements need to be thoroughly understood and followed if patients are involved or if there is an intention to publish the results.

Step 4. Develop a program plan, budget, and timeline, and identify funding sources.

These detailed plans should be approved by the full committee and submitted to executive decision-makers for review and approval.

Possible funding sources should be identified. Funding may come from a sponsoring department, general operations, a private donor, or a grant. Participatory and performing arts programs generally are not funded out of capital or operating dollars; they are usually funded from either designated or undesignated philanthropic dollars or grants. Visual arts programs are generally funded through a combination of philanthropy and capital dollars.

Healthcare institutions usually approach the financing of arts projects with various strategies, including the following:

- Funding the design of the program internally and finding philanthropic dollars for its execution, installation, and maintenance.

- Funding the program from organizational dollars with a goal of recouping a percentage of the costs from philanthropy.

- Funding the entire program, including design, from philanthropic dollars. This is sometimes accomplished with a small seed gift of $5,000 to $10,000, which allows an institution to bring together an internal team and an external consultant to create the scope, budget, and schedule.

Rady Childrens Hospital
Artist: Dennis Smith

The financing of visual arts programs is very similar to funding bricks and mortar through a capital campaign. It is best to design the program, develop a case statement for it, and create a plan for locations and descriptions of artwork for which the organization is seeking sponsorship. It is appropriate to have renderings for some of the larger proposed pieces, showing them in location for presentation to a particular donor. A funding booklet can be created that offers all of the funding opportunities for visual art in a manner similar to the way areas of a new or remodeled facility are offered for funding in a capital campaign.

Breaking down an overall visual arts program into defined dollar amounts assists the foundation in finding the appropriate donors to support individual programs.

Some Ways of Measuring Project Outcomes

The projects described in this book illustrate a wide range of methods for ascertaining whether a project has accomplished its purpose or purposes. Among those methods are the following (all measurement strategies should be developed in conjunction with experts and in conformance with all organizational and ethical standards):

Physiological tests. Blood cortisol levels and other serum indicators are measured to assess stress reduction; heart rate, blood pressure, and other indicators are also used (see *Arts at the Bedside* and *Bedside Harp* for examples).

Motor-skill assessment. The participants' ability to perform certain physical functions can be used to assess the success of rehabilitative interventions (see *Virtual Music Maker*).

Observed behavioral outcomes. Where the project goal is to affect specific behavior, the participants' behavior can be observed to see whether the outcome was successfully achieved (see *Pediatric Procedural Support*).

Standardized written self-report questionnaires. Questionnaires have already been developed to assess many of the factors toward which some arts interventions are directed. For example, the Hospital Anxiety and Depression Scale (HADS) is widely used to measure those characteristics in patients (see *The Dreams Art and Health Project*).

Custom-developed written self-report questionnaires. Carefully designed instruments can be created to ascertain from participants' responses whether a project's desired outcomes have been attained. There are many projects in this book that use such instrumentation, including *MusiCure, 203 Days, BOOM, Strange Gifts,* and *The Firefly Project*.

Interviews with participants. Using a structured protocol, participants can be asked to respond to questions that reveal whether the project has successfully attained its goals (see *Prenatal Therapeutic Dance Project*).

Observation by outside experts. Experts unrelated to the project can observe the participants and evaluate whether the goals have been achieved (see *Arts Access*).

Observation by skilled project "insiders." Project staff or others associated with the project can conduct structured observation of the effects of an intervention (see *Music Therapy in Palliative Care*).

Spread of ideas. Some projects, such as *Health Through Art*, aim to increase awareness of health issues among certain populations. Their effectiveness can be assessed through surveys and other methods (such as focus groups) for determining how extensively and accurately their message has been received.

Each gift should have donor recognition, either in the annual report or within the facility, such as a separate arts donor plaque or a plaque hung beside a work of art that describes the particulars about the artwork and gives the donor's name.

Step 5. Train, inform, and supervise artists.

Gail Ellison leads a writing workshop at Shands Hospital, University of Florida Health Science Center, Gainesville, Florida.

All regularly-performing artists and participatory artists should be trained by an organization that prepares artists to work in healthcare settings – such as the Society for the Arts in Healthcare or one of its recommended organizations. Most healthcare organizations have a training program for volunteers that artists must attend before being allowed to work there. Participating in such a program informs the artist about general rules and regulations for working at the facility as well as about appropriate communication with patients and families.

Artists' activities should be carefully managed: for example, they should check in with a designated manager when their shift begins, and they should document each event or interaction with a patient. For participatory projects, a monthly review should be held among arts administrators, artists, and the clinical partners to ensure that the project is on target, that training is adequate, and that the process is appropriate. For example, at the University of Florida's Shands Hospital, the artist-in-residence program is monitored through a program called "Artist Rounds," in which artists meet once a month with artist mentors and clinical team representatives to discuss the individual efforts of the artists-in-residence and to learn from each other.

Step 6. Communicate widely within the organization about arts programs.

When an organization shows its support for well-chosen, well-designed arts programs, ideas blossom. There are often many people in many parts of healthcare organizations who can identify low-cost, high-impact opportunities within their own areas of responsibility. The organization can demonstrate support for encouraging innovative ideas through communicating about the arts program in official publications such as newsletters and reports, and on the organization's website.

St Joseph Mercy of Macomb, Clinton Township, Michigan
Artist: Tama Dumlao

Scripps Mercy Hospital Chapel,
San Diego, California
Artist: Mario Uribe

Step 7. Conduct outcome studies.

Outcome studies are essential and do not have to be expensive. Artists can collaborate with researchers from within the institution, from a higher-education institution, or from an arts agency. Hospitals generally have many volunteers and academic institutions have graduate students who are eager to do meaningful work. They can be trained to collect data.

The costs of outcome studies should be identified and included in the original project budget, to help ensure that they are not eliminated at the end of the project. Many music and artist-in-residence programs are funded by individual grants that require annual reporting for continuation of their funding. To support this reporting, evaluation information should be diligently collected and reviewed. An agreed-upon measurement instrument should be consistently used.

Step 8. Improve and expand the program as appropriate.

Build on success. A project that is effective in one location within an organization might have applications elsewhere. Or, it could be that the general principle of an effective intervention could be extended to other functions. For example, upon finding that music therapists provided an effective way to relax children before noninvasive tests, Tallahassee Memorial Hospital applied music to increase relaxation in other potentially stressful situations, such as the insertion of an IV catheter.

Improve on shortcomings. If a program that has produced good results elsewhere isn't working as well as expected, make sure that all aspects of implementation are being handled as they should be. Regular monitoring, feedback, and discussion, as described in step 5 above, can allow for corrections while a project is ongoing and also provide a wealth of information for decisions about improving – or abandoning – the project when those decisions need to be made.

Scripps Mercy Hospital Chapel
Artist: Tama Dumlao

Step 9. Publicize results in peer-reviewed journals and other outlets.

An organization that implements projects in the way we have described can contribute significantly to its own reputation and to the field at large. Evaluations can be published in journals such as *Health Environments Research & Design Journal* and *International Journal of Arts and Medicine.* Nursing journals and specialized clinical journals by practice areas are also excellent ways to reach healthcare practitioners and others.

Experiences and results can be presented at national and regional conferences such as the national conference of the Society for the Arts in Healthcare, arts therapies conferences, and design conferences such as the Center for Health Design and the Healthcare Facilities Design Symposium.

At a minimum, organizations should post their results on their websites and distribute press releases describing the results of their arts programs. Published stories by patients or employees who have benefited from an arts program can be very effective.

Conclusion

High-impact arts programs do not just happen. They require collaboration between the artist and the organization, designed to achieve agreed-upon objectives. The nine-step process described here provides a good roadmap for any organization that, if followed, will increase the likelihood of success.

---

1. www.healthdesign.org

2. www.thesah.org

Collaborating with the Community in Arts Programming

Increasingly, healthcare institutions are finding innovative ways to partner with community institutions through the arts.

For example, many health centers are incorporating stages into certain areas to allow performing arts groups to come into the facility; the performances are often recorded and then broadcast to patients who are unable to attend in person. On a volunteer basis or for a nominal honorarium, a very broad range of individual and group performers can be engaged to perform at healthcare facilities. A part-time or full-time arts coordinator can screen potential performers, orient them to the facility and its expectations, and schedule and manage the performances.

Since many museums keep up to 95 percent of their art collections in storage, artwork can often be obtained on a long-term loan basis from local museums of art, history, natural history, and science. There are challenges to exhibiting museum-quality art, but it is manageable with the right partnership attitudes. Similarly, local art organizations often have, or can arrange, collections for display at a facility.

In arranging for performances and exhibits, it is important for the healthcare institution to heed its stated mission and goals so that this does not become an exercise in art for art's sake. The guidelines for effective art and performance established by current research (as discussed in chapter 2) must be respected, so that what is presented to patients and visitors will do no harm and genuinely contribute to the quality of the healthcare experience.

Laura Corlin performs at St. Jude Children's Research Hospital. *Photo by Pat Corlin*

"Imagine if all healthcare organizations used the arts to reduce anxiety, fear, and fatigue while providing inspiration and hope to recover and renew.... The arts alone will not cure cancer or prevent strokes, but they significantly improve the care experience. Creating such environments is within our reach. Let us find the wisdom, creativity, compassion, and commitment to make this happen in our communities and throughout the world."

– page 209

Conclusion and Recommendations

Healthcare leaders, artists, and healthcare consumers all have important roles in transforming the healthcare experience through the arts.

St Joseph Mercy of Macomb
Artist: Austine Wood Comarow

At a time when core issues about healthcare are being debated, one thing seems certain: the current healthcare system is not sustainable economically. Whatever changes are adopted and implemented, appropriate use of the arts can and will make an important positive difference for all stakeholders in the system.

In addition to economic reform, we believe that four major trends will influence which healthcare organizations survive and thrive in the years ahead. First, the arrival of the "baby boomers" as major consumers of healthcare cannot be ignored. They represent a major attitudinal shift from passive patients to outspoken consumers. In addition to expecting highly-trained healthcare professionals and state-of-the-art technology, this new generation of patients can be expected to demand that the care they and their loved ones receive will be provided in a pleasant, calming environment. *The arts have a role here.*

Second, the shift from reliance on word-of-mouth referrals and the general brand name reputations of healthcare organizations to publicly-mandated patient satisfaction scores gives consumers unprecedented opportunities. For the first time, they will be able to make healthcare choices based in part on readily available, fully comparable reports of the experiences of other consumers that are transparent and widely available. *The arts have a role here.*

Third, the healthcare safety/quality revolution that began a decade ago has become mainstream. The Institute of Medicine's six domains of quality – safety, efficiency, effectiveness, timeliness, equitability, and patient-centeredness – are now well known throughout the healthcare industry and are becoming widely recognized benchmarks of good care. *The arts have a role here.*

Fourth, the field of evidence-based design continues to grow. Similar to evidence-based medicine, there has been a significant and sustained growth

Scripps Memorial Hospital, San Diego, California
Artist: Dianne Seabeck

in the number and diversity of published articles that show the connection between well-designed healing environments and improved healthcare safety and quality for patients, families, and staff. Some of this research focuses on actual healthcare impacts while others focus on the perceived experience by patients of their care. *The arts have a role here.*

This book is intended to help healthcare leaders better understand the healing arts and what they can do. In addition, we have described the differences between arts therapy and arts programming, and we have provided many case examples that show the healing, calming, and uplifting results that occur when an inspired artist is engaged by a committed organization.

Throughout this book, we make connections between the worlds of healthcare and the arts by building bridges of understanding based on actual experiences. We have had the privilege of taking you on a journey of 36 stories that describe how a variety of innovative artists have worked with extraordinary healthcare leaders to produce remarkable results. These pioneers have shown us new vistas of what is possible when creativity and compassion work hand in hand, side by side. They provide beacons of hope in an uncertain and often scary world of healthcare.

Musicians preform as part of the *Art for Recovery* Healing Garden Music Series.
Photo by Karen Gehrman

RECOMMENDATIONS

Individuals and organizations are improving lives through the arts. Let us follow in their footsteps. Accelerating the adoption of these programs will require three things:

> *Healthcare leadership teams* **with a strong vision of integrating the arts into new expansions, remodels, and existing programs.**
>
> *Artists* **who are called to this field and become partners with healthcare organizations.**
>
> *Healthcare consumers* **who want to have art experiences for themselves and their loved ones while they are going through challenging times.**

We offer the recommendations below for each of those groups.

Healthcare Leaders

We have shown how arts applications can provide high-impact, low-cost means of addressing key institutional goals that include improving patient and staff satisfaction, improving the experience in waiting rooms and emergency departments, reducing pain and anxiety for patients, developing new community collaborations, improving the experience of the physical environment, and finding new funding opportunities and new donors. Leaders who recognize this opportunity are urged to consider the recommendations that follow. Those who do not yet recognize the opportunity are urged to maintain an open mind and continue educating themselves about the potential for increased effectiveness that the arts provide.

Exempla Good Samaritan Medical Center
Artist: Carol Schneider Fennell

1. Educate your board through best-practice examples of how well-designed, properly-implemented arts programs can support the strategic goals and key initiatives of your organization.

2. Develop a multi-year plan that describes how the arts will support your overall goals and needs.

3. Start small with projects that have a good potential for success.

4. Allocate a fixed amount of your capital improvement budget for the arts.

5. Involve your foundation and seek new donor sources. Art programs should not compete with healthcare programs or technology. Develop a strategic plan for raising money for the arts.

6. Develop collaborative partnerships with local arts agencies, councils, museums, and art schools. Healthcare organizations are creating valuable partners in their own communities with resources, talent, and expertise to provide services to their constituents.

7. Conduct outcome studies and publish the results.

8. Communicate the impact of your programs internally and externally; celebrate your successes.

9. Advocate for insurance reimbursement for art and music therapies that have been proven to work.

10. Advocate for more government support of the arts in healthcare.

Artists

This book shows how knowledgeable, committed artists can collaborate with healthcare organizations to transform the experiences of patients, visitors, staff, and others. Consider the following recommendations:

1. Participate in training programs for artists working in healthcare environments.
2. Intern in an established arts and health program.
3. Study what has been proven to be effective, learning from information on the internet and in published sources.
4. Join the Society for the Arts in Healthcare.
5. Learn about your local healthcare facilities' arts programs.
6. Learn about the healthcare organization you want to work with and see how your arts program could support its strategic initiatives.
7. Develop concrete ideas for programs that are your passion. Prepare a scope of work, timeline, and budget, and find out who are the advocates for similar programs in your local healthcare institutions.
8. Collaborate with art consultants working in healthcare.
9. Learn about funding opportunities available through the Society for the Arts in Healthcare and other sources.
10. Advocate for healthcare art classes in art schools.

Consumers (patients and families)

Learn about the arts programs in your local healthcare organizations.

1. Use the availability of arts programs as one of the criteria that you apply in selecting a healthcare organization.
2. Join patient advisory groups to advocate for the arts and communicate the importance of arts programs.
3. Write to your political leaders about the importance of funding the arts in healthcare.
4. Find out how you can volunteer or financially support the arts in your healthcare organization.
5. Write letters of support to senior healthcare leaders about positive encounters you have had with the arts within their organizations.
6. Share information about the potential of the arts as a valuable complementary therapy with your family and friends.

Scripps Mercy Hospital
Artist: Mary Lynn Dominguez

A Final Thought

Virtually anyone who has had a positive art experience while going through the healing journey becomes a convert to the value of integrating effective arts programs into the healthcare experience. Many doctors and nurses who witness the impact of the arts on patients and their families are forever changed.

The arts are not the first thing that people think about when they are ill, worried, and stressed. When brought to them lovingly, it is usually a surprise, a caring moment reminding them that there still is beauty, delight, and hope.

Imagine if all healthcare organizations utilized the arts to reduce anxiety, fear, and fatigue, while providing inspiration and hope to recover and renew. Imagine if this became the standard of care everywhere. The arts alone will not cure cancer or prevent strokes, but they significantly improve the care experience. Creating such environments is within our reach. Let us find the wisdom, creativity, compassion, and commitment to make this happen in our communities and throughout the world.

Lyn Sanders and staff, Matheny Medical and Educational Center

Afterword

Roger S. Ulrich, Ph.D.
Professor of Architecture, Texas A&M University,
and faculty fellow of the Center for Health Systems & Design

During the past decade, the field of evidence-based design has come of age. It is now widely recognized that well designed physical environments play an important role in helping to make hospitals less risky and stressful for patients, families, and staff.

It is less well recognized and documented that the visual arts, music, dance, and storytelling also make important differences in reducing patients' anxiety, lessening pain, aiding in their recovery, and improving their overall experience. This outstanding and ground-breaking book is a major step in changing this. It presents a splendid diversity of stories and case studies of real partnerships between creative artists and innovative health care organizations that have helped to improve outcomes and the care experience. These examples show us what is possible.

The authors also provide an excellent discussion of the pressures health care organizations face today and how the arts can help to address some of them. They present a clear nine-step process that any organization can undertake to design, implement, and sustain effective arts programs. These sections are important for enhancing the practical usefulness of the book.

The authors also review published research studies involving a variety of arts interventions and a diverse range of patient populations. From my own research in hospitals in several countries, I have seen first-hand the important impact that carefully designed arts programs have on patients, their families, and staff. I applaud the book's call to action for more research on the effectiveness of various types of arts interventions in different care settings.

This well organized, well written, and beautifully illustrated book merits serious consideration for selection as assigned reading in schools of architecture, design, medicine, nursing and health care administration. Congratulations to Blair Sadler and Annette Ridenour for providing this valuable contribution that can help improve the healthcare experiences of so many around the world.

An example of a comprehensive health policy regarding the arts and health can be found in the United Kingdom:

Department of Health Policy

Arts and health are, and should be firmly recognized as being, integral to health, healthcare provision and healthcare environments, including supporting staff. The arts are, and should clearly be recognized as being, integral to the quality of the experience for patients and service users, and to supporting healthcare staff. They make a major contribution to improving people's lives, their health and healthcare provision, providing high-quality, appropriate healthcare environments and engaging with individuals and wider communities, including hard-to-reach groups. Given the connections between communities, participation, education, health, employment and well-being, there are opportunities for the Department of Health and the NHS to use the arts to bring about change in some of the key influencers of health and in the use of the NHS.

– from "A Prospectus for Arts and Health," Department of Health with Arts Council England (2007)

Appendices

Monoprint from the *Dreams Art and Health Research Project*, Mater Hospital Trust, Belfast, Northern Ireland

"The artist does not draw what he sees, but what he has to make others see."

– Edgar Degas

Appendix A *Artist and Institution Contact Information*

Alexander, Marlene
marlena@bendbroadband.com

Art for Life Foundation
www.artforlife.org
staff@artforlife.org

Art with Heart
www.artwithheart.org
info@artwithheart.org
(206) 362-4047
Steffanie Lorig:
steffanie@artwithheart.org

Arthur, Christine
pinkpainteddaisy@yahoo.com
(812) 323-7680

Arts Care
www.artscare.co.uk
artscare@cinni.org
028 9053 5639 (Belfast, Northern Ireland)

Barash, Bailey
www.bbarash.com
bbarash1@cs.com
(404) 373-8246

Bridgman, Melinda
m.bridgman@snet.net
(860) 928–6515

Buchanan, Renée
renee-buchanan@uiowa.edu
(319) 512-9590

Carr, Janet Lew
see Danceworks

Children's Cancer Association
www.JoyRx.org
office@JoyRx.org
(503) 244-3141
Emily Hoffmann:
ehoffmann@joyrx.org
(503) 200-5117

Cleveland Clinic, The (Harry R. Horvitz Center for Palliative Medicine)
www.clevelandclinic.org/palliative
Lisa Gallagher:
gallagl@ccf.org
(216) 445-5083

Corlin, Laura
lauracorlin@gmail.com
(603) 664-9983

Danceworks
www.danceworksmke.org
Janet Lew Carr:
jcarr@danceworksmke.org
(414) 277-8480 ext. 6010
Deborah Farris:
dfarris@danceworksmke.org
(414) 277-8480 ext. 6000

Duncan, Jane
www.publicartanddesign.com
jpduncan@publicartanddesign.com
+44(0)777 9322236 (London)

Dykehouse, Jeff
www.emilysbigpictureproject.org
jeff@emilysbigpictureproject.org
(616) 446-6263

Eje, Inge
see MusiCure

Eje, Niels
see MusiCure

Elkan, Edie
www.bedsideharp.com
(215) 752-7599
edie@bedsideharp.com

Ellison, Gail
gail@gailellison.com
(352) 870-4323

Engel, Judy Nguyen
judynengel@gmail.com

Appendix A *Artist and Institution Contact Information*

Farris, Deborah
see Danceworks

Friedman, Judith-Kate
www.songwritingworks.org
director@songwritingworks.org
www.judithkate.com
(360) 385-1160

Gallagher, Lisa
see Cleveland Clinic, The

Geist, Margot
Geistlight Photography
www.geistlightphotography.com
margot@geistlight.com
(505) 243-2316

Ginsburgh, Judy
www.artsandhealthcare.org
(318) 769-7602
judy@artsandhealthcare.org
(318) 442-8863

Hastings, Lorna
see Arts Care

Hoffmann, Emily
see Children's Cancer Association

Hyatt, Liza
www.lizahyatt.com
lizah2@lizahyatt.com
(317) 823 -0370

Jones, Chamira
www.chamirastudios.com
(313) 530-7708
Chamira@chamirastudios.com

Kenny, Tisha
www.healththroughart.org
(510) 549-5990
tishakenny@att.net

Lahav, Amir
lahav.email@gmail.com
(617) 632-8914

Lorig, Steffanie
see Art with Heart

MAP Foundation, The
http://mapfoundation.org
Info@mapfoundation.org
01273 873014 (Brighton, England)

McDonald, Kyle
mcdonaldkj@aol.com

McGinn, Bridget
see St. Charles Medical Center

Meyer-Miner, Anne
annemm19@gmail.com
(505) 867-2981

Modlin, Robin
robin@dreamdancerdesigns.com
(650) 494-3714

MusiCure
www.MusiCure.com
contact@musicure.com
+45 45854948 (Copenhagen, Denmark)

Pediatric Procedural Support Program
see Tallahassee Memorial HealthCare

Perlis, Cynthia
Cynthia.perlis@ucsfmedctr.org
(415) 885-7221

Reider, Susan Wood
www.honorthejourney.com
swreider@honorthejourney.com
(603) 226-6416

St. Charles Medical Center, Bend, OR
www.cascadehealthcare.org/Bend/
(541) 322-4781
Bridget McGinn
bmcginn@cascadehealthcare.org

Sanders, Lyn
www.artsaccessprogram.org
lyn@artsaccessprogram.org
(908) 234-0011 ext. 440

Appendix A *Artist and Institution Contact Information*

Schillaci, Patricia Caballero
ps2188@columbia.edu
(212) 729-3401

SEEWALL Studios
www.seewallstudios.com
(843) 476-7435
rocco@seewallstudios.com

Tallahassee Memorial HealthCare/
Florida State University
musictherapy.fsu.edu/tmh/
Miriam.hillmer@tmh.org
(850) 431-7468

Thiessen, Linda
www.artcare.ca
(604) 941-8091
lthiesse@sfu.ca

Walsh, Sandra M.
swalsh@mail.barry.edu
(305) 899-3810

Wellesley, Rosanna
rosie_wellesley@yahoo.co.uk
+44 (0)7813162633 (London)

Winterbottom, Daniel
nina@u.washington.edu
(206) 612-1146

Appendix B *Resources*

Aesthetics, Inc. (www.aesthetics.net) – This internationally recognized team designs public and community arts programs and creates arts and healing environments for healthcare institutions. As a leader in the field, they have installed over 100 programs nationwide.

American Art Therapy Association (www.arttherapy.org) – Its mission is to serve its members and the general public by promoting standards of professional competence and developing and increasing knowledge in the field of art therapy.

American Dance Therapy Association (www.adta.org) – This organization is dedicated to the growth and enhancement of the profession of dance/movement therapy and to promote and provide resources for dance/movement therapists.

Americans for the Arts (www.americansforthearts.org) – This organization is dedicated to representing and serving local communities and creating opportunities for every American to participate in and appreciate all forms of the arts.

American Music Therapy Association (www.musictherapy.org) – Music Therapy is an established healthcare profession that uses music to address physical, emotional, cognitive, and social needs of individuals of all ages.

Arts and Healing Network (www.artheals.org) – An online international resource for anyone interested in the healing potential of art, especially environmentalists, social activists, artists, art professionals, health care practitioners, and those challenged by illness.

Art for Healing (www.artforhealing.org) – This organization provides works of art, which enhance the quality of life for the ill, their caregivers, and loved ones.

Creativity Matters: The Arts and Aging Toolkit (www.artsandaging.org) – This resource explains why and how older adults benefit from participating in professionally conducted community arts programs.

Foundation Center (www.fdncenter.org) – Recognized as the nation's leading authority on organized philanthropy, connecting nonprofits and the grantmakers supporting them to tools they can use and information they can trust.

International Networking Group of Art Therapists (www.internationalarttherapy.org) – Its mission is to increase international networking and information exchange with particular interest in reducing the isolation of colleagues attempting to advance the profession of art therapy single-handedly.

Appendix B *Resources*

Midwest Arts in Healthcare Network
(www.maihn.org) – A coalition of health-care providers, artists, and community members working together to integrate the arts into the world of health and healing.

National Association for Drama Therapy
(www.nadt.org) – A membership organization that provides resources on drama used for therapy.

National Association for Poetry Therapy
(www.poetrytherapy.org) – NAPT members have forged a community of healers and lovers of words and language. They work in many settings where people deal with personal and communal pain and the search for growth.

National Center for Creative Aging
(www.creativeaging.org) – The National Center for Creative Aging (NCCA) is dedicated to fostering an understanding of the vital relationship between creative expression and the quality of life of older people.

National Coalition of Creative Arts Therapies Associations
(www.nccata.org) – This organization provides an alliance of professional associations dedicated to the advancement of the arts as therapeutic modalities.

National Endowment for the Arts
(www.arts.endow.gov) – The National Endowment for the Arts is a public agency dedicated to supporting excellence in the arts, both new and established; bringing the arts to all Americans; and providing leadership in arts education.

National Network for Arts in Health Canada
(www.artsinhealth.ca) – Arts In Health works within hospitals and healthcare environments with hospital administrators and clinical staff to utilize and understand the value of the arts in enhancing well-being.

Performing Arts Medicine Association
(www.artsmed.org) – PAMA is an organization comprised of dedicated medical professionals, artists educators, and administrators with the common goal of improving the health care of the performing artist.

Society for the Arts in Healthcare
(www.thesah.org) – This organization is dedicated to advancing arts as integral to healthcare.

VSA Arts (www.vsarts.org) – VSA Arts is an international, nonprofit organization founded in 1974 by Ambassador Jean Kennedy Smith to create a society where all people with disabilities learn through, participate in and enjoy the arts.

Directory and Index

Directory and Index

"Surround Yourself with Good Stuff"
Artist: Eric Peterson

"I believe we're all called to be healing. I believe in the creative pulse that makes beautiful warm quilts from scraps of wornout clothing, poems and song from the words we use every day, organizations for social change out of nothing more than the promises we make and keep with each other. And we're called to celebrate."

– Mary Pellauer

Directory
The Arts Projects and Programs in this Book

The 36 case examples in this book are listed here by the primary type of arts intervention employed in each. Some projects are listed in more than one category.

Index

Index

Index

About the Authors

Annette Ridenour
is President and founder of
Aesthetics, Inc., a 30 year old
healthcare design firm, based
in San Diego. She has built
an international reputation in
collaborating with healthcare
institutions to bring harmony,
balance, and beauty to the built
environment through art programs,
architecture, interior design, and
graphic design. She is a recognized
leader, consultant, and lecturer
on evidence-based regional
arts programs that reflect the
vision and values of healthcare
organizations. Annette is also
a co-founder of Aesthetic Audio
Systems, Inc., implementing music
programs for healing, therapeutic,
and environmental improvements
in healthcare settings.

Annette has served as board
member and president of the
Society for the Arts in Healthcare,
and is the 2006 recipient of the
Janice Palmer Award. She currently
serves on the Advisory Board for
The CARITAS Project.

Blair L. Sadler, JD
is a Senior Fellow at the Institute
for Healthcare Improvement,
and a member of the faculty at
the UCSD Schools of Medicine
and Management. He served
as President and CEO of Rady
Children's Hospital in San Diego
from July 1980 until July 2006.
Under his leadership, Rady
Children's was the first pediatric
hospital in the United States
to win the Ernest A. Codman
Award for its work in developing
clinical pathways. He speaks to
healthcare boards of trustees
about their role in patient safety
and quality.

He served on the board of the
Center for Health Design, and
has been heavily involved in
developing the business case for
building better hospitals through
evidence-based design. He has
consulted with several health
systems throughout the world
regarding building optimally safe
and low stress hospitals through
evidence-based design.